In a Wonderful Lifetime

**A Biography Of Albert Minshall And
The Hill Valley Golf Club**

by Gillian Lee

Published by

Albert James Minshall
Hill Valley Lodge
Terrick Road
Whitchurch
Shropshire
SY13 4JZ

Tel: 01948 666994

First published in Great Britain in 2008 by Albert James
Minshall, Hill Valley Lodge, Terrick Road, Whitchurch,
Shropshire, SY13 4JZ

Printed in Great Britain
Design and Layout by Partnership Publishing Limited
2 Crown Street
Wellington
Telford
TF1 1LP
Tel: 01952 415334

Contents

PART ONE
From The Beginning To The Opening Of Hill Valley Golf Club 1933-1975

PART TWO
Hill Valley Golf Club

PART THREE
Family, Friends, Faith and Charity

PART FOUR
The Future at Hill Valley Golf Club

Foreward

I have known Albert for over forty years, both as a friend and business associate. At one point we owned over twelve different businesses, as diverse as building, hairdressing, garages, DIY shops, wrough iron and breeze block manufacturing, clothing boutique and fishing tackle.

Albert's attitude is that the glass is always half full, never half empty. His enthusiasm for life flows over into whatever situation he finds himself in, whether it is business, sport or family orientated.

His first and foremost priority has always been his family followed closely by his strong religious beliefs; I am proud to be God Father to his youngest son, Andrew and Albert is God Father to my son Michael. He has always fully supported Michael in his career as a professional golfer, taking time out to watch him play all over Great Britain and Europe.

Sport has always played a major role in Albert's life, eventually fishing, cricket and football gave way to golf in the mid-sixties and following his venture into the golfing business, as one of the syndicate of twelve businessmen who purchased Hawkstone Park in 1966, he then decided to build Hill Valley Golf Club.

Over the years many people have asked me about Albert, and to sum him up, I'd say that he can always see the good side of everyone, he never sees any bad, and this mind set, along with his enthusiasm for life, has seen him enjoy a very successful family, private and business life.

Albert's generosity has helped many people privately without any recognition and for over fifty years his company have provided a Christmas party for more than 100 local senior citizens and I know many eagerly await their invitations.

Long gone are the days when he carried on in business to make money, these days his pleasure is from seeing other people enjoy the facilities he has built.

Les Welch

Introduction

Hill Valley Golf Course

"From the championship tees the course plays a full 6884 yards whereas when the club members play the course for their club medals it is 6601 yards long. The par 72 is fair but not easily achieved unless a great deal of thought and care is taken. The eighteenth hole is particularly memorable, demanding a long straight drive to the plateau green guarded by two mature trees and two ponds."

"It's a good life if to get to do what you want to do."
Albert

"You see it's all a dream. You don't get to have too many dreams in your life. I won't get another one now, I certainly won't get one at my age. The dream was there. Hill Valley was the dream and it's never changed. It's still the dream for me today as much as it was all those years ago.

Maybe it came to me because I was at a crossroads in my life where things could have gone drastically wrong with too much time on my hands and other things that you could get into that could be wrong. It was given to me. It's given me a good life, I've always been happy. Financially it's probably the worst thing I ever did but it's also been the happiest thing I ever did. I've missed out on a fortune in property developing where I began my working life. I would have been better off without a golf course. But I'm differently rich, rich in so many ways. There's a difference between finance and happiness. I've had 30 years of hard work and happiness, maybe I'm not as rich, but I can sleep at night. If you're happy in your job and reasonably well off, well, what more can you ask?

If I had any sense I'd sell up and go and retire peacefully but I won't because it's still my dream.

People playing on the Hill Valley golf course think it's their course. It's as much their course as mine. You can't own anything in life. You're just a general manager for a while. We're all on this earth together, just running around on a big ball and that's it."

Albert James Minshall

Hebrews 13: 5-6

Keep your lives free from the love of money and be content with what you have, because God has said,
" Never will I leave you; never will I forsake you.
So we say with confidence,
" The Lord is my helper; I will not be afraid. What can man do to me?"

PART ONE

1st Tee:

Albert James Minshall
Earliest Days In Shropshire
From Bricklaying . . .

1st Hole - Par 5 - 471 yards

An inviting tee shot just the fairway bunker on the right to avoid on the otherwise generous fairway. A good tee shot will leave a fairway wood or long iron in to the long green protected by three large greenside bunkers and a pond to the lower left hand side of the green, a good hole to pick up a birdie on.

"If you find where you're looking for in Whixall, having only asked somebody for help once, then you've done very well. Most people ask a chap the way and half an hour later they come across the same chap from another direction and ask him all over again. Whixall is like that."

Cyril Forrester, Whixall

EARLIEST YEARS

Albert James Minshall was born into a very quiet corner of rural North Shropshire on 26th August 1933. The village of Whixall, large in area but tiny in population, managed to evade the urbanisation of England's countryside in the twentieth century and remains still rural in the 21st century. It is still very easy to get completely lost amongst its maze of narrow winding roads that jigsaw around the tranquil canals and ancient peat mosses. In 1933, the gathering of peat, along with the farming of the land, was a main industry in Whixall. Today the mosses are peaceful wildlife havens, a designated SSSI site and cared for by English Natural Heritage.

Albert lived in Moss Lane with his parents Victor and Beatrice, his brother John and sisters Rosie and Connie. He looks back on a happy, wholesome childhood filled with a lot of love. His father had a pig dealing business so he also remembers a lot of pigs. School did not suit him very well and he showed little interest in academia, preferring to tend the school garden for the headmaster, Harry Green.

Mother, Rosie, Grandmother,
Connie, John and Albert

When his parents moved to Moss Farm he showed even less enthusiasm for farm work.

"Looking back, I realised my heart was in a different place than on working farms. It was my father's chosen path for me but I didn't think I could be as successful as he had been. I must have been about twelve or so when I began looking for something else to do with my life. Anyway, one day our house needed a new roof."

That was the chance that lit the spark for the years ahead in Albert's life. Harry Preston and Sons of Whixall, a local builder and family undertakers, was commissioned to renew the roof of the farmhouse.

"Watching the men set to work intrigued me as a young thirteen year old and I began to give the lads a hand."

He immediately knew that this was what he wanted to do and he never returned to lessons. He went to work for J. Preston and Sons.

Victor and Beatrice   *Albert*

Albert watches brother John

FROM BRICKLAYING . . .

"Here at Preston's I learnt my trade. It was Raymond Preston who taught me to lay bricks, plaster walls, the art of joinery, decorating, paper hanging and door hanging. It was a wonderful training which set me up for life."

Norman Peate, known as Peachy, a cousin of Albert's was also apprenticed to J. Preston and Sons. Norman and Albert were born within a fortnight of each other. They began Whixall primary school together on the same day in 1938 and both left school and joined Preston's.

NORMAN PEATE

Norman Peate

"We've been together ever since we were born. We played together as children and then we played football for Whixall and cricket for Coton together, we went out to the pubs together. We even began our National Service and were de-mobbed on the same day although we were in different regiments. I was sent to Aldershot. It might as well have been America it felt so far away. I had never been out of North Shropshire. As soon as we both had leave we would get together again and then we worked together for years. We've never really been apart. We thought the world of one another and still do. He's always very placid and I'm the opposite. I can get all heated and he just smiles and walks away and I always thought that was one of the best parts about him because he never held anything against us and if anything was wrong he'd be there like a flash, he couldn't bear it no matter who's fault it was. Right from the beginning Albert was a naturally good bricklayer and tradesman, he learnt quickly and took to it all. In those days everything was done manually, there were no mechanical diggers. It was all done by us, shovelling and digging and mixing and carrying everything with our own hands."

Proverbs 3: 1-2

My son, do not forget my teaching, but keep my commands in your heart, for they will prolong your life many years and bring you prosperity.

Albert remembers one incident,

"Very early on in the days of our apprenticeship I was returning to the builders yard one afternoon when up comes Peachy on his bike carrying six bricks in the basket."

"What're you doing?" Albert asked him

"Well, we've got this job up the road," replied Peachy, "but we're about thirty bricks short, so I'm taking some back."

"Six at a time?"

"Six at a time," he replied.

"Well, I'll give you a hand."

"No, no, you're all right." Peachy said.

"Well, where's your mate, can't he help you?"

"No. He's busy."

"Doing what?" I asked.

"Well, whatever he's laying it's not bricks!"

After three and a half years with Preston's, an opportunity came along which Albert seized. A local Whixall farmer, Chris Allman, required a new cow house and offered Albert the job.

Albert had £24 to his name that he had saved after six months of bricklaying. After the cow house he was asked to build a garage. Instead of making £4 a week, now working for himself, it was closer to £40. One year later, he built his first house.

John Anderson, Tony and Beryl. Albert's first Rolls Royce, 1975

Ecclesiastes 4: 9-10

Two are better than one, because they have a good return for their work: If one falls down, his friend can help him up. But pity the man who falls and has no one to help him up.

2nd Tee:

National Service. 1951-1953

2nd Hole - Par 4 - 405 yards

Blind tee shot over the crest of the hill with a dominant oak tree bounding the left hand side of the fairway, but don't leak the shot off to the right as the fairway falls away over a mound into trees, once the fairway is found a mid to long iron should find the back to front sloping green with a large bunker wrapped around the left hand side.

"When the call for duty came, I wasn't exactly ready, but nor did I run a mile."

Albert

Albert had a feeling that he would be 'hopeless' in the army and wondered where in the world he would be posted; he was quite happy when he found it was to be to the Kings Shropshire Light Infantry in Shrewsbury, just eighteen miles from home.

The first six months at Copthorne Barracks were hard. It was his first time away from home, his family, and all his passions: football, fishing, cricket and his trowel. But Shrewsbury had one big attraction: girls.

"It was often a sight to see my khaki uniformed body going over the barrack wall to meet some local girl in town. It was the same khaki uniformed body that would consequently be put on a charge and confined to barracks the next day."

After six months Albert was transferred to the 66th Artillery Regiment in Yorkshire. Soon after this transfer there was a turning point for the young lad from Shropshire and National Service took a turn for the better.

"Anyone here from Shropshire?" barked a Sergeant at roll call one morning.

"Yes sir."

"Where are you from?"

"You won't know it Sergeant."

"Go on son, where're you from?"

"Place near Whitchurch."

"Where?"

"Whixall."

The Sergeant looked down at his roll call sheet, looked back

12

up at Albert, "Do you know Victor Minshall?"

It was the start Albert needed and with the mentoring of the sergeant who knew his father, Albert progressed to Lance Corporal. In order to receive a second stripe and become a Corporal, a 'second class' education certificate was necessary which Albert did not have. With encouragement from the sergeant Albert gained this certificate and was promoted to Corporal.

The third stripe, promotion to Sergeant, was achieved soon afterwards and within his two years of service. This speed of promotion was rare in those times but then he lost it almost immediately. To celebrate his promotion to Sergeant a night out at the pub was arranged.

"The celebrations possibly got a little out of hand. I can't remember too much about it other than ending up asleep in the road in the gutter and being woken by the car of the commanding officer of the 66th Artillery Regiment. I was back to serving as a Corporal by lunchtime."

One month later the regiment moved to London for the coronation and the stripe was returned.

The most memorable occasion during Albert's National Service days was being on parade for the coronation of Queen Elizabeth II. Kensington Gardens had become a sea of tents to accommodate the forces and Albert's regiment was amongst them.

Albert (on the far right) during National Service.

Many of those who couldn't actually be in London on that day gathered around any television set they could find. In London, the grand and sumptuous enthronement ceremony drew unprecedented crowds who, wanting to leave behind the bleak

13

years of post war rationing, arrived and were filled with excitement, ready to herald in a new, modern era with hope.

"But for me, it was something of a nightmare. As a newly re installed sergeant I was in charge of a platoon of sixty men. Every part of Her Majesty's forces were represented on parade down the mall. Everyone was shouting orders and counter orders which became very confusing and I lost half my men."

But it was a day he has never forgotten.

Albert third from the right.

The young lad from Shropshire, who felt he wasn't 'worthy' enough to be a sergeant and had hardly ever been out of Whixall, now reflects, with the benefit of hindsight, that his two years in the National Service, undergoing the strict discipline of army training, the expectations it demanded of him and being catapulted out into the wider world from his safe and isolated home village, was the best thing that could have happened to him and set him up well for many different challenges in the years ahead.

"I never would have stood the stresses and strains through the years of building up my business, without that discipline and training."

The army were keen for him to stay but Albert was keen to get home.

HOME AGAIN

Coming home to Whixall after completing his National Service was a relief for Albert and he threw himself back into his work and life, just as much as before it had been interrupted, when he had been called away from it all.

As well as working hard, Albert returned to play hard at the sports he loved. He set about all of them with the same dedication and vigour he gave to developing his business career. He played football for Whixall and Wem for many years and cricket for twenty years for Coton Hall Cricket Club.

Albert as goalie for Wem Town.

Albert in goal for Whixall.

He also had a passion for fishing and spent any spare hours he could on the banks of the North Shropshire and Welsh rivers and streams.

For a young man in Shropshire in the 1950's there wasn't too much to do at night. Albert and his mates would wander around dressed in the fashionable clothes of the day that made them look quite villainous. The clothes of the youths today attract as much negative social comment.

"Yet nine times out of ten, these people, as in my day, are sound, decent human beings. I have found over the years that appearances can be deceiving. It makes me think the old proverb: 'Never judge a book by its cover' is very true."

Most weekend evenings were spent at local village hall dances dressed in full drape suits and crepe shoes.

"I knew Beryl from the dances I went to at Prees and Wem. But she was wise even then and wouldn't have anything to do with me as I looked like a rogue and was nearly always drunk. In my eyes she was the prettiest girl of the lot and I wouldn't give up and eventually Beryl decided to let me take her out."

Everything went well, except the unfortunate incident when Albert drove Beryl's mother to Shrewsbury for a day of shopping and the front wheel fell off the car.

"The car wasn't made for only three wheels and we finished up in the ditch. That didn't go down too well with Beryl and her mother but fifty years later with five children and twelve grandchildren they have forgiven me. In 1956, with my brother, John, as best man, Beryl and I were married at the Whixall Far End church and now we have just celebrated our 50th wedding anniversary and are still happy and good friends which is the most important thing in any marriage."

Alberts wedding picture, August 1956, 50 years ago

Beryl and Alberts wedding

Proverbs Ch31 Vs 10:

Who can find a virtuous woman? for her price is far above rubies.

3rd Tee:

The Foundations Of Albert's Building Business

3rd Hole - Par 4 - 411 yards

Tee off over the crest of the hill to a large fairway. The better player will hit a fairway wood off the tee and try and hug the right hand side of the fairway for a better approach to the green. A mid to short iron should be a comfortable choice into the Plateau green protected by two pot bunkers at the front and fierce slopes at the rear.

"Throughout his early years he exhibited a strong desire to reach high standards of achievement whether it was in his business or leisure activities."

Tony Parsonage

"I first met Albert playing football for Whitchurch Allport Reserves against Whixall at Whixall and this spindly youth was playing in goal for Whixall. We used to change in the Waggoners Pub."

Bob Walker

Returning home from National Service in 1953 Albert immediately started working back in the building trade getting a job with a very good builder called Harold Ward. Harold was building new houses in the Edstaston and Wem districts and it was very good experience for Albert and his future.

"Harold was a very nice man and treated me like his own son. He put me back in good stead to go into house building. After that I went to work for one of the most likeable men I have ever met and probably one of the most successful, Charlie Brown of Brown's of Whixall. He built portable buildings all over Europe. My job for the short time I was with him was to look at problem buildings, buildings which were odd shaped or weren't square. I remember finishing one house, where I had had to rebuild the roof and it was a foot wider at one end than the other. I drive past that house these days and it still looks pretty good. I'm the only one who knows that one end is wider than the other. We always endeavoured to complete a job satisfactorily!"

He soon knew he wanted to start building for himself again.

Albert was discussing his ideas with his cousin Norman Peate one day in the lane in Whixall when they met John, Albert's brother.

"I'm thinking of starting a building firm. Would you put £1000 into it?" Albert asked John.

"You must be joking!" John replied.

Albert's chance came when his mother and father decided the farmhouse was too big for them and they wanted a new bungalow.

"I took the job on and other than the electrics and plumbing I built and completed the bungalow myself."

After that the work began to come in constantly and Albert's own building business really began to develop rapidly. Norman Peate joined Albert on his first bungalow and remained with him for the rest of his working life.

NORMAN PEATE

"We started with a shovel, a barrow and an old van. There was an old shed down at his father's farm and we would store building materials in there. I used to bicycle 3 miles over to Albert at the farm every morning. We would work all day on one job, have a quick tea and then take on another job in the evening before finally having a pint at the very end of the day. We worked long hours and we worked hard."

When Albert and Beryl married in 1956, they went to live in a self contained apartment at Moss Farm where his brother John lived with his wife in the main house. John ran the farm and Albert developed his building business.

John and Albert got on well all through their lives. Only eighteen months older than Albert, John always seemed to be the more sensible lad, who fairly frequently rescued Albert from trouble as a youngster.

"Looking back, I was a bit wild and John was always the sensible one who bailed me out."

On several mornings John remembers his mother asking him where Albert was as she had only heard one set of feet coming home and up to bed late in the night. John would tell his mother that Albert was quite safe and in bed. His mother was always right, she had only heard one set of footsteps and that was because John carried his brother home and safely up to his bed.

On another occasion when Albert accidentally tipped his car into the local canal, he came home and told John what had happened and then promptly fell asleep. John stayed awake all night worrying about it for him.

There was plenty of land at Moss farm and as each successive job ended the pile of left over materials grew and so it became a builders yard.

Albert and Beryl had never intended to stay at Moss farm for very long so after a short time he bought a plot of land in Whixall about half a mile away and began to build a new bungalow.

"I built it mainly at nights after work with one or two of the local lads coming to give me a hand. The one thing that does stick in my mind, it happened in those days but not so common nowadays is that I had more money in the bank after I finished the bungalow than when I started. The main benefit is that we never had to have a mortgage. I think we've moved house thirteen times now and each time I've managed to fall lucky in that I've always sold the house at the right time."

One day Albert saw a plot of land for sale in Station Road in Wem. After a bit of negotiation he bought it and got permission to build eight houses. He had only just got the money to buy the land and begin the building work.

"My father and I didn't always see eye to eye on the business. He didn't think that I was responsible enough to build speculative houses. But one day I went to the bank to fix up some money for the building work and the bank manager told me, "You're all right for money Albert. Your father has just put £3000 in the bank."

Alberts first bungalow.

Victor, his father, having thought Albert was mad, had had

second thoughts about the venture after talking with Beryl who had told him that she didn't think that Albert was mad at all and he knew exactly what he was doing.

Some days later Victor was passing the site and found Albert digging out some footings.

"Do you think you'll ever sell these houses, son?" he asked.

"I've already sold 'em," replied Albert and he was able to re-pay his father just three months later.

Victor was a strict Methodist who did not approve of drinking, in particular his son Albert drinking. But they enjoyed a wonderful and loving relationship that developed and grew ever stronger as the years passed.

Norman: "More and more projects came along and A.J. knew how to do everything from laying the bricks to ordering materials but what he also knew was how to pick his men and how to treat them and deal with all the wages. He had the knack of getting the right men for the job and was good at talking with them."

Albert: "Peachy was really good when it came to finishing all the jobs off. It was his job to do all the final bits so we could get our money off the customers. I suppose you'd describe him as a general foreman in those days."

Norman: "I used to work out all the money at the end of each week in the early days when we were quite tight and I used to worry about telling Albert if we had any money left over because he'd go off and buy another bit of land or a building. But you see 99% of the time he'd get it right and it would be a good investment or development. He had a golden touch. It hasn't surprised me one bit that Albert has done well because he was never afraid to take a gamble. He had a knack of buying just the right piece of land or building, he had good vision, good foresight about what places to buy and things to develop. And good luck of course. I would have never have got anywhere without him because I would never have taken those chances."

Norman became a director of A.J. Minshall Ltd in 1962. It was he who kept the business going during the worst of Albert's illness in 1964 when he was completely confined to bed and during his subsequent slow recovery. A.J.Minshall Ltd expanded each year and completed many major and diverse building projects from garages to offices, shops and schools and the building of many hundreds houses in Wem and district. In 1972 Norman decided to remain with the building side of A.J.Minshall Ltd and not become involved in the development of Hill Valley.

Norman: "It would have been too much for me, I would have gone to bed and worried. Albert, he goes to bed and goes to sleep. That's why we made a good partnership, no use both being the same. Albert can relax better than me."

Luke 12: 25 -26

Who of you by worrying can add a single hour to his life? Since you cannot do the very little thing, why do you worry about the rest?

4th Tee:

Albert's First Round And The Discovery Of The Game Of Golf

4th Hole - Par 3 - 196 yards

An uphill demanding par 3 that even the best of players hit a long iron into with a long green protected by two large bunkers either side.

"That little white thing controls you."

Tony Hateley

It was during his National Service days that Albert first came across the game of golf. As he was walking with a mate across the links of Sherringham Golf Club in Norfolk a golf ball came flying towards them landing near their feet. The other chap picked it up and threw it into the sea. A few seconds later a lady and a gentleman stopped close to where the ball had landed.

"That was their ball," Albert said.

"No point in telling them now, is it?" replied his mate.

The couple, who both looked in their eighties and were resplendent in plus fours, spent a long time searching for their missing ball. Through the years of searching for stray golf balls that moment has always stayed with Albert; it was his very first brush with golf and what not to do when you find a golf ball on a course.

FIRST GOLF GAME: BLACKPOOL

The first time Albert held a golf club in his hands was at the age of twenty-three in 1956. He was on holiday in Blackpool, the popular Lancashire seaside resort, staying at the Norbreck Hydro Hotel. It was suggested one morning that a game of golf would be a good idea. The course chosen for the family game that morning was not the Royal Lytham St. Anne's nor Fleetwood but the course attached to the Norbreck Hotel. Sadly the hotel course is no longer there having been swallowed up under housing estates. Albert was the only non-player in the group and didn't have a set of clubs. The manager of the hotel, a kind man, offered to lend Albert his own set. Albert set off happily with this arrangement but realised almost immediately as he held his first golf club in his hand that he would need a left-handed set. Arrangements were quickly made to borrow a left-handed set from the manager of the nearby Carlton Hotel and so began his first ever game of golf.

That same week Albert also played at Stanley Park nearby. The fourth tee was a short hole of 120 yards and Albert chose a wood to drive the ball straight from the tee onto the green where it landed into the middle of a group of four golfers putting. They were reasonably annoyed and so Albert had his first lesson in etiquette. Since that moment Albert has played thousands of games of golf on many different courses but thirty five years later, standing at the fourth tee at Stanley Park again, playing in a competition, his caddy gave him a wedge, until he remembered the events at that hole all those years ago clearly. That day marked the beginning of a journey learning the etiquette and honesty that is required of anyone playing golf. The etiquette, honesty and discipline needed for golf are a good metaphor for the highs and lows of life in general.

"It's easy to move a ball, even six inches, while no one is looking but you're just cheating yourself."

What he also recalls clearly is that the manager of the Carlton Hotel got his clubs back. In the years since then, Albert has lent three sets of clubs and three electric golf trolleys out to the visitors of Hill Valley. It was only the last man to borrow a set who returned them. That man restored Albert's faith in human nature for he now believes that at least one third of the human race is honest.

Those first two games of golf did not instil an instant passion for the game. That took a few more years. Albert played football and cricket to a good village green standard and had a great love for those sports. After that first round in Blackpool, Albert picked up the occasional club and had the odd round of golf, mostly when on holiday with his sister Connie and brother in law, Frank Cartwright.

In 1964 Albert was taken fairly seriously ill. Since completing National Service he had worked hard and put in very long hours building up his business. He had continued to play sports hard, enjoyed his drink* and had a young family. Something had to give and it was his health. He was completely laid up for a few weeks and there followed a long recovery period.

"I certainly wasn't as fit as I used to be and it was a good many years before I got back to feeling what I would call 'right'."

But Albert was keen to throw himself back into everything he had had to put on hold. It was his wife, Beryl, who suggested he try golf as an alternative to some of the more arduous physical sports.

*Albert gave up alcohol from this time onwards.

HAWKSTONE PARK GOLF CLUB

Hawkstone Park Golf Club was situated only five miles from Albert's business in Wem. Albert wondered if not only would he be really suited to golf but would the golfing world allow him in?

"I don't know whether I'll fit in with the golfing set."

Beryl, knowing Albert's love for sports and his have a go personality replied, "Oh go on, get on with you. Go and have a go at it. You never know, you might even like it!" She eased his fears, assured him they were financially well off and that he was capable of playing as well as many others who played.

So with this cheerful encouragement Albert set out on this new challenge in his life and went to see Alex Lyle who was the professional at Hawkstone Park in North Shropshire. He paid a £10.00 subscription, then left promptly to go to Shrewsbury to buy half a set of golf clubs not realising that the professional shop at Hawkstone stocked clubs.

The 1960's golfing fraternity was made up almost wholly of professionals, the landed farmers and gentry and Albert's doubts about being welcomed in to this 'club' and being accepted by the members were, after all, unfortunately well founded. He found he waited for long periods hoping to be invited to play golf. It was Alex Lyle, the professional at Hawkstone Park golf club who encouraged him to persevere and slowly he began to play more regular games. Albert remembers Alex Lyle as a courteous and gentle mannered golf professional who looked after all the visitors and players with great care and consistency. It was Alex, with his gentle and encouraging teaching manner, such as quietly altering Albert's grip, that helped Albert settle and progress rapidly and very soon he was recognised as a good player, competing at all levels.

"He was wonderful to me in those early days and he never changed."

It was now that a passion for the game of golf took a firm hold on him. It became so intense that Albert played almost every day for two years, which while bringing his handicap down to four in 1966 could have engulfed his home life and business. He needed to achieve a balance with this new passion; to manage his love for playing golf and be able to play to a standard that he felt happy with and not risk neglecting the demands of his thriving business, his health and his wife and family. He needed a balance that would work for everyone.

He achieved more than a balance. With quite breathtaking acumen he managed to amalgamate all three elements that were the passions of his life: golf, business and his family into an inclusive whole during the next phase of his life.

He also never forgot those difficult early social experiences at a golf club. The impressions they left stayed with him and played their part years later when the vision of his own much more inclusive golf club was born.

Ecclesiastes 9:10

Whatever your hand finds to do, do it with all your might.

5th Tee:

Golf In The USA And UK 1933-1972.
By Tony Parsonage

5th Hole - Par 5 - 524 yards

The most demanding of par 5's on the course, a tee shot over the crest of the hill in to a generous fairway, but precision of the shot is imperative as the second shot over the pond is defended by poplar trees on the right and left hand sides, most players usually hit a long iron to lay up on the right hand side of the fairway three bunkers protect the green which slopes fiercely from front to back and putts from the back of the green have to be treated with the upmost care.

"People ask why has England done so well with golf? Albert's dream was not just to build a golf course. Thirty years ago, when he built Hill Valley, there was a totally different attitude to youngsters. They were only just tolerated at many golf clubs. They were only allowed to play after 4pm on weekdays and at weekends. But Albert broke the code. He was a pioneer. He foresaw the need to encourage the youngsters, to encourage the natural swing they have and that this was the way forward. Now he allowed Woosie to play in a Peter Alliss trophy senior tournament. Woosie was my bottle up boy at the time. He had that vision, for a boy to win a man's competition."

Peter Condliffe

When Albert arrived in this world in 1933, King George V was King of England and the Empire, Hitler was Chancellor of Germany. Franklin D. Roosevelt was President of the U.S.A. and prohibition ended in America after fourteen years. Sasha Distel, Roman Polanski and Fay Weldon were born. Sir Malcolm Campbell broke the world land speed record in Bluebird at 272m.p.h. Arsenal was the major football power in the country, Gordon Richards was champion jockey, the world heavy-weight boxing champion was the Italian Prima Canera and the England Cricket team undertook the controversial 'bodyline' tour of Australia.

Golf as an emerging world sport was in its infancy.

Great Britain and Ireland won the Ryder Cup. Bobby Jones and Clifford Roberts decided to hold a golf tournament at Augusta for their friends; the first Masters was held in 1934 and won by Horton Smith.

There were only six 18-hole golf courses in Shropshire, Shrewsbury, Oswestry, Church Stretton, Ludlow, The Wrekin and Hawkstone Park

Television was not available to the general public, beer was less than a shilling (five pence) a pint and a packet of cigarettes were a shilling for twenty.

Very few people had more than a very limited knowledge of golf although newspapers and the wireless had been recording the achievements of Bobby Jones, Walter Hagen and many other famous American golfers. In Britain, it was Henry Cotton who stood out as the predominant player, and had 'raised eyebrows' by breaking away from the old traditional image of the professional golfer. That tradition ensured that the 'Pro' was everything from green keeper, bar steward, club repairer and locker room attendant. Professionals were rarely even allowed into the clubhouses of the day and few of them ever got the time to play the game itself. Occasionally they would 'obtain permission' from the club to play in a professional event, but there were very few of these events at that time. Even then the tournaments always finished on a Friday, so that the professional could return to serve the Members at the weekend. It's not surprising that the standard of golf in Britain lagged sadly behind the American game.

Little changed in Britain in the 1930's and during the war many golf courses were requisitioned for military use or simply neglected. These had to be recovered and rebuilt after the war and yet still there was no change to the restrictive and traditional nature of the game's structure. Members Clubs with their selective membership criteria, archaic rules and regulations did nothing to encourage the expansion of the sport in any way.

It was the Americans who propelled the sport on to new levels after the war. They did not have the shackles of the restrictive social class hierarchy that stifled development opportunities in Britain. The majority of golf courses in Britain were owned and run by Members' Clubs, and without gaining membership it was difficult for those people who might have wanted to play to gain access.

The press and wireless still rarely reported golf events so there continued to be little interest and very limited understanding of the sport among the mass population. In the post war years and well into the 1950's the view persisted that it was an elitist sport, played mainly by professional businessmen, the wealthy and rather dowdy ladies. During the 1950's the achievements of the renowned professionals, South African Bobby Locke and Australian Peter Thomson dominated the domestic gamc, winning ninc Open Championships between them. Their fantastic exploits were followed avidly in the golfing world and in the U.S. Ben Hogan and Sam Sneed were creating headlines and widening the pool of interest to a greater audience. Travelling to Britain these two legendary golfing figures both won the Open Championship and together won the Canada Cup, the forerunner of today's World Cup.

In the late 1950's two things happened which acted as the catalyst needed in Britain to propel the game forward and generate mass interest.

The development of television outside broadcasts was crucial in exposing awareness of the game to a much wider audience than ever before.

At exactly this time, onto the golfing scene burst the man who probably bears the most responsibility for the massive worldwide expansion and interest in golf that it enjoys today - Arnold Palmer.

If any one man lit the fuse that set off the world-wide explosion in golf it was Palmer. He burst upon the scene in a manner and style that caught the public imagination as no one before him. He was the embodiment of the 'nice guy next door' and yet with a presence about him that could leave the most senior businessmen, traditionalists and others almost tongue-tied in his presence. However, Palmer's respect for the traditions of the game itself and his sportsmanship became by-words wherever he travelled and set the standards expected from the new generations of golfing enthusiasts

Throughout the early 1960's the golfing achievements of Arnold Palmer together with Jack Nicklaus, Gary Player, Lee Trevino and other great American golfers dominated the professional game and were seen by millions of people on television across the world. The public appetite for golf and its increasing exposure on television to the growing numbers of people who had access to television were the fortunate and crucial factors that merged at that point in history.

THE BEGINNINGS OF CHANGE
IN GREAT BRITAIN

Suddenly, in the late 1960's, a young working class lad from Scunthorpe burst onto the scene and started to win championships that until then had been for years in the sole possession of professional golfers from the U.S.A. and other parts of the world. Tony Jacklin won The Open Championship in 1969. His performances, as he went on to win The US Open Championship, two Jacksonville Opens in Florida and numerous other major events around the world were inspirational. Here was a young British player taking on the best players in the world and at long last competing more than favourably. His success and the image he projected served to further motivate a large potential golfing market in the UK. Now the real problem was evident for all to see. Jacklin's wonderful achievements inspired many people who were eager to play themselves, but where? There had still been little expansion in the facilities available, all the traditions and restrictions were still in force and the great numbers of people now wanting to take up golf were unable to do so. Even if they did they were faced with the same dogmatic and elitist practices that had frustrated Albert in 1964 when he arrived at Hawkstone Park Golf Club.

A survey carried out at the time by the golfing authorities clearly indicated that as many as 700 new golf courses were required to satisfy the demand. The rush to build Golf courses was on, but it was essential that new facilities were developed that provided the opportunity for anyone to play without the old fashioned restrictions of Club Memberships. The concept of Pay & Play, where anyone could roll up, pay a green fee and play on good golf courses was the answer.

It was against this background that Albert was forming his own ideas for the future of golf. He had been successful in business, he had gained valuable experience with his involvement at Hawkstone Park and he had the resources to drive plans forward to meet his dream of, 'Providing first class golfing facilities for everyone at reasonable prices.'

Proverbs 16:3

Commit to the Lord whatever you do, and your plans will succeed.

6th Tee

Business And Golf Merge.

6th Hole - Par 3 - 187 yards

From the tee only the right side of the green can be seen at 187 yards a mid to long iron is the club but don't pull the shot to left as water behind the green protects the hole from the over ambitious player, also be wary of the road that runs in front of the green.

"I can only work with people who are positive. I can't work with anyone who is awkward or negative."

Albert.

"It was at this time, in 1964, that Beryl said that the business was getting too much for me and perhaps I needed some help."

Norman Peate was still working for Albert and there were also two girls in the office but it was really an office manager that was needed.

LES WELCH

 Albert: "I rang the up the technical college in Shrewsbury to see if they might have anyone promising. The head there said that he had a lad who lived out at Tetchall, near Ellesmere, who he thought might be suitable and so Les Welch came to see me and he was good, very good."

After a couple of weeks Beryl asked Albert how the new young lad was getting on?

"I can't seem to find him enough work to do. I give him a job and as soon as my back's turned he's finished it. It's beginning to worry me," Albert replied.

"Well, this went on for another couple of weeks and then I thought I'd try him out on pricing the building jobs. Work was coming in daily and again it was getting too much for me to do on my own. Yet again he seemed to find a knack of doing this. His prices weren't too far out and before much longer he didn't have too much time on his hands.

"Les worked hard for us so we bought him a little Mini which was fine, but when you consider Les is six foot three inches tall

31

when he drove around his legs seemed to be wrapped around his ears. We decided to give his knees a rest and bought him a bigger car."

In 1968 Albert and Beryl made Les a director of the company and gave him 10% of the shares. The partnership between Les and Albert developed rapidly and by the early 1970's Les became a director of several companies that Albert had either bought or started and Managing Director of A.J. Minshall Ltd., the head company that was funding the capital to buy and start all the other companies.

Les had left school at fifteen and spent a few years in the Merchant Navy, travelling around the world. He then joined an architect's office in Oswestry where he gained an invaluable training for his future career when Albert made the telephone call that was to transform his life.

HAWKSTONE PARK

John Wade owned Hawkstone Park and one evening in February 1967 he asked Albert to go and see him. John wanted Albert's joinery lads to make some packing cases for some oil paintings at Hawkstone.

"These paintings were about eight feet by six and I should imagine they were worth about £25.000 each back then. I looked at these paintings and I just felt that the responsibility was too great for us and he should get a professional packing company to do the job. Anyway our conversation carried on and he suddenly said,

"I'm selling the place, you know."

"Oh ay," I said, "what, the lake as well?"

"Yes," he replied, "the whole lot."

Albert asked him how much he wanted for the lake. John repeated that he wanted to sell the whole place. Five minutes later he offered the lake to Albert for £5000. Albert made a different offer. In the end the deal was done and they settled on £4250. Albert had bought the lake he had taken delight in seeing from his first visit and had kept in mind for good local fishing, especially in the early days in case his golfing adventure had not turned out so well.

Some time later, Albert passed the title of the lake to the local Angling Club, who years later were reputedly offered £1 million for the same sporting lake.

John then asked Albert about the rest of Hawkstone Park. Albert had just bought thirty-five acres of land to build 150 houses on so his money was already tied up in that project.

"This is how life is so unpredictable; you just don't know what's going to come your way."

Just eighteen months later, after the completion of the housing project, Albert could have bought Hawkstone Park in its entirety out of A.J.Minshall Ltd quite easily, "But that's life!"

The day after Albert purchased the lake he was playing golf with Alex Lyle, Chris Simpson and David Evans on the course at Hawkstone. On the eighteenth fairway Albert mentioned the possibility that Hawkstone Park would be for sale. Alex confirmed this and mentioned his concern for his own future as a professional at Hawkstone.

"I was only trying to cheer him up when I said it wouldn't be impossible to buy the place. Looking back I think Alex was worried about having to uproot his family and possibly leave Shropshire. He had children who were interested in the game. I think he was anxious to keep a steady hand on their progress. That was the type of man he was."

They decided to make more enquiries.

"It was Chris Simpson who suggested that we form some sort of syndicate to buy the place. Although I had just bought the lake I knew I could find enough to buy a share in a twelve-man syndicate. Both Chris and Alex could find the money and David Evans was keen and certainly the wealthiest man amongst us. By eleven thirty that same evening we had twelve men that formed the syndicate to buy Hawkstone Park, the last being Edward Bygott, the solicitor. He was wonderful and did a lot of the work for free, which he did for us until we sold in 1988."

The twelve men offered £4250 each. The property had been valued at between £70.000-£75.000. With a small amount of borrowing the deal was completed by midnight the same night. The Hawkstone Park (Successors) Ltd announced their purchase at the beginning of February 1967; it was confirmed on March 8th.

The young man, who had arrived rather tentatively and then waited so patiently to be invited to join with others in games of golf at Hawkstone Golf club, now only three years later, could call the entire place, in part, his own.

Albert introduced his own children to golf and Tony Minshall and Sandy Lyle played a lot of golf together over the subsequent years.

SANDY LYLE

"I remember Albert all those years ago when he and my father became part of the twelve-director syndicate who bought

Hawkstone Park. Albert was a big name locally in building and he had achieved great things in Shropshire that were impressive at the time. His son, Tony, was keen on golf and being local lads, we played a lot together. I was at school with Tony's sisters in our rural, quiet part of the country and it was always exciting when Albert was around because he would arrive enthusing about the newest ideas or the latest pieces of equipment being developed for golf at that time.

He was eager to learn but he also wanted to involve us in it all too, he was generous with this enthusiasm, keen to share it with us and he made it good fun. He would bring along some newly developed graphite clubs and encourage all of us to have a go. He would find out the latest ideas in golf coaching and talk about where we should go and what to do. At the time everything was happening in America and the availability of information wasn't there for us as it is now all over the world. The ideas and influences were gradually coming over here but we were living right 'out in the sticks' and it was refreshing that someone was bringing all this to us and we saw and felt a little part of the forefront of golf as it was developing in those years. If you wanted to know anything about the latest fashion in golf or fishing Albert was the man! He introduced me to fishing as another sport to enjoy apart from playing golf."

Barry Ralphs, Alberts's caddie in the 60's and 70's.

Albert remembers playing golf with Sandy Lyle at Hawkstone Park.

"I remember Sandy's first days playing golf and he was about four years old with his cut off golf clubs. From his very earliest days he concentrated hard on his game. He was a fantastic boy player who went on to win the British Open in 1985 and U.S. Masters in 1988 and is still playing well today. We played many games together through his teenage years. He was always a lovely lad who loved his music and also always kept a smart appearance. I played a few holes with him at Hill Valley after he won The Open and he's still on great form and I'm sure he will win some senior tours."

Alex Lyle and Albert played many games together including the Shropshire and Herefordshire Alliances. (1960-1970) They, along with their co-directors of the Hawkstone syndicate, enjoyed many good days and had fun over the years.

His business, A.J. Minshall Ltd, was by now well established and prospering. In 1969, with a good eye for opportunity again, he bought 57 acres of land at Wemsbrook Farm near Wem from John Gittins for £1000 an acre. Planning permission was obtained to build residential houses and just twenty acres of this produced a tenfold return on the original investment. This provided Albert with the means to progress when the next opportunity came along.

Albert's interest in Hawkstone Park was unwavering but he recognised that there was a huge market in golf that could be tapped. There was certainly little opportunity at Hawkstone alone to cater for the rising demand for facilities in North Shropshire. New courses needed to be built and he began to look for suitable opportunities that would meet this need so that he could develop his dream. He knew now exactly what he wanted to do.

Enthusiasm, opportunism, youthful energy, business acumen and challenges were the ingredients that drove Albert.

"Little did we know, that in buying Hawkstone it gave Les, Norman and myself the invaluable knowledge and experience we would call on when we decided to buy the land to build Hill Valley."

Proverbs 20:13

Do not love sleep or you will grow poor; stay awake and you will have food to spare.

7th Tee:

The Buying Of Two Farms: Hill Valley Is Born.

7th Hole - Par 5 - 501 yards

The tee shot here requires you to carry the ball over two streams onto the fairway guarded both left and right by trees. Players will then attack the green over another stream with a fairway bunker on the right hand side. The better player will take the green on in two but with a bunker on the left hand side and another on the right wrapping round to the front of the green the entrance is quite tight.

"I was never really one to miss an opportunity and perhaps the greatest opportunity that ever came my way was in 1972."

Albert

Hill Valley farmland.

"It began as a morning like all the mornings before. I arrived at work one November morning, at 7.30 am and Norman Peate was giving out the building jobs to all the men and seeing them on their way. Then I went up to the office to meet Les and iron out any problems. Maybe I had reached a crossroads in my life. I had been in the building trade about twenty years and

36

it was very successful. We had built houses and schools and lots of other general building work. I think I was a bit bored and looking for something new and different. I used to sit on the windowsill over a radiator. At about 9.0'clock I was sitting there watching Les working hard as he always did and I started thinking about an article I had seen in the Whitchurch Herald, our local weekly paper, about planning permission for a golf course. I wondered if the land was up for sale because no one had begun building a golf course.

"Just hand me the telephone," I said to Les, "I'm just going to check on some land in Whitchurch that has got planning permission for a golf course."

Les was quite happy with the idea as he was keen on golf and he and Albert played together at Hawkstone. The first call was to Albert's brother in law, Frank Cartwright.

"He told me to ring the local auctioneer, Horris Stokes. He was a very well known man locally and well liked and a good character in his time. He was the perfect man to work with and to set up a deal."

Hill Valley farmland.

Fifty minutes later and by ten o'clock in the morning, after only one more phone call, Albert was standing on the land that was for sale and there he met Harold Bateman, the farmer who owned the land with planning permission.

"I asked him whether the land had got full planning permission and he told me it had, so to save a lot of argument I offered him £1000 an acre. Land back then was worth about £300 an acre but it had got planning for the golf course so we shook hands on the deal and settled for £180,000 for 180 acres."

The following day Les went to see the farmer who owned the eighty-acre farm next door to the Bateman's. This farmer, John Ellis, also wanted to sell his land. He was offered the same price, £1000 an acre and so twenty-four hours after reading about the first farm, Albert has purchased not one but two farms.

They recognised that they had stumbled on an outstanding site for a golf course. The two farms were set in a gently rolling landscape just 20 miles from Chester and 50 miles from Liverpool, Manchester and Birmingham. The land had a rich growing soil that covered a huge bank of sand, providing perfect drainage combined with the ability to grow good grass quickly from seed. As he wandered out and looked at the landscape he had bought, Albert knew that these 260 acres were the perfect land on which he could build his vision of a major championship quality golf course and club. His vision was to build a course equal to anything in the area and to even rival some of the great courses in the British Isles. At that time, proprietary golf complexes were almost exclusively confined to the affluent counties of the south and this made Albert's plans in the North Shropshire all the more visionary.

Proverbs 37:3-4

Trust in the LORD and do good: dwell in the land and enjoy safe pasture.

Delight yourself in the LORD and he will give you the desires of your heart.

8th Tee:

The Development of Hill Valley: 1972-1975

8th Hole - Par 4 - 434 yards

Stroke index 1 on the card and arguably one of the toughest par 4's around. Tee off from the slightly elevated tee and thread the ball between water on both sides of the fairway but too far left and the second shot becomes blocked out by the dominant oak tree, once on the fairway the second shot with a mid to long iron is over a pond that stretches from the front of the green completely round the right hand side, further danger lies on the left with two treacherous deep bunkers. If you leave over the buckle bridge here with a par you will have done well.

"To provide first class golfing facilities for all who want to play and enjoy golf at reasonable prices. Albert had a clearly established philosophy for his dream."

Tony Parsonage

THE DESIGNERS

Peter Alliss and David Thomas were both Ryder Cup players of distinction.* In the late 1960's, realising the rapidly growing demand, they formed a business partnership to design and construct golf courses. Albert, with his desire for excellence was keen to commission them to design the course for him on his farmland.

"I rang Peter Alliss one morning and engaged his firm to design the new course."

Albert and Beryl arranged to fly to Southern Spain and meet the distinguished designers in La Manga. They wound their way by car over miles of dusty track to a remote restaurant in the hills. There, they met Peter and David and with much local wine and traditional Spanish food, they sat in the shade and began their plans for the design and construction of the golf course in Whitchurch, England. Albert knew they were not only very good players who had represented their country but were very knowledgeable and he liked their ideas. They agreed a fee and it was the start of a long friendship.

Peter and David came and walked the 260 acre farmland to survey the ground and then produced sketch plans that included a further nine hole golf course and a nine acre practice area on land on the other side of Terrick Road. With Albert's business, A.J.Minshall Ltd, able to supply earth moving and construction equipment the course developed rapidly.

Albert wanted to build the course first followed by the clubhouse. He and Les went with their wives to Marbella in Spain for a holiday where they sat on the beach drawing up plans for the clubhouse and a hotel. The planning department in Shropshire, however, insisted on some major changes so Peter Roscoe and Chris Bean from Shrewsbury were employed as architects and the ideas formed on the beach in Marbella were reluctantly 'scrapped'.

"Ah well, such is life." Albert muses today about it all, although he still feels some regrets that the courtyard feature that he and Les had designed would not only have been better but also that their plans to build on flat ground would have been much less costly than the final version.

The new clubhouse, built into a bank using re-enforced concrete was expensive. It was very modern and included bars, restaurants, hotel accommodation, a function room and indoor leisure facilities including snooker.

THE NAMING OF HILL VALLEY.

Albert had decided to name the new course St. Alkmunds, complimenting the name of the parish church in Whitchurch. But after much debate the contradictory name 'Hill Valley' was chosen because the land is set on a hill interlaced with valleys. Magnificent views stretch over the Cheshire plain to the foothills of the Welsh mountains and six counties in all including The Wrekin, Church Stretton and beyond.

THE FIRST PRESS CONFERENCE
FOR HILL VALLEY

And so on a grey, bleak day in October 1973 Albert and his managing director Les Welch, summoned the golfing press and a number of other close friends to a press conference at The Victoria Hotel in Whitchurch. Around a hundred people attended. Peter Alliss and David Thomas were there. Representing The Professional Golfers Association was Tony Parsonage, a former Shropshire and Herefordshire champion. At that time he was the senior Tournament Administrator for The P.G.A. and had known Albert and Leslie for some years. Tony was very interested to see the fruition of this exciting new plan in his home county. He was hoping that Hill Valley could become a venue for future professional tournaments. His hopes came true. Within its first year, in July 1976 Hill Valley hosted the Midlands Open, repeated in 1977 and followed by a sponsored £3000 pro-am tournament and Hill Valley has continued to host officially recognised P.G.A. events every year.

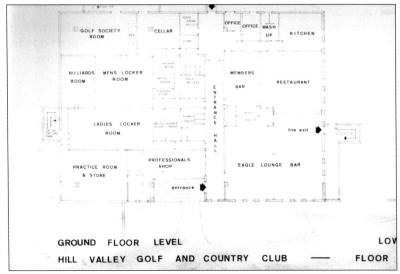

First plans for Hill Valley Golf Club.

Albert stated that, "We are hoping to attract not only experienced golfers but to get a lot of people playing who have never held a golf club in their hands... Our aim is to give everyone good value for money and to create a real and happy club atmosphere."

Most of those who attended that evening at The Victoria Hotel became founder members and many more joined quickly. The first member's diary booklet in 1976 listed 271 members and membership increased up to 400 within the first year of opening.

Peter Alliss became an internationally renowned golf commentator. He frequently mentioned Hill Valley, both on the BBC and American television, whether it was to report the current playing professional or just for fond memories and he often sent personal messages through colleagues.

Construction began in February 1974 and by April 1975 after complete re-seeding the course was playable. With only slight alterations the original 6884 yards, par 72 course designed by Peter Alliss and David Thomas is still there today.

"I don't think I could have found two better people to design a golf course. They designed a great course and now even

41

thirty years later Hill Valley is a testament to both Peter and David. They made a very good job of the design and then we also did all the work ourselves. There was very good quality sand there already. We took peat from our home farm in Whixall and made sand and peat greens. There aren't many of those in the country. It wouldn't be allowed today."

Architects drawing for Hill Valley Golf Club.

The rich growing soil, combined with the sand and peat, allowed Hill Valley course to feel immediately more mature with fairways as good as other courses achieve only after many years and greens which even in December hold fast. Mature existing trees were preserved and natural water hazards were already lying in over half the holes. The hole left after removing the peat from Whixall was made into a fishing lake that is sometimes used for televised fishing programmes.

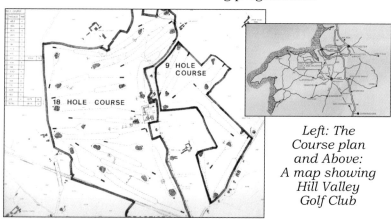

Left: The Course plan and Above: A map showing Hill Valley Golf Club

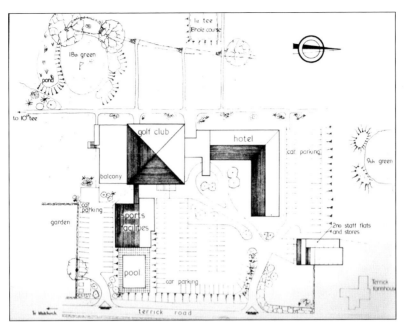

Plans of Hill Valley Golf Club.

In 1975 THE SPORTS REPORTER, DAVID DAVIES WROTE:

"Out there, deep in the heart of Shropshire, something stirs. In fact it more than just stirs, it blooms, and that is a £1 million development of a golfing complex that is already one of the finest of its kind and promises to get better.

Hill Valley Golf and Country Club is the complex, Whitchurch the rather unlikely situation and three self made men its creators..................

It has in my opinion at least four holes to rank with the best, which is a high proportion for any course and considerable credit to its two designers, Peter Alliss and Dave Thomas.

The finishing hole on the championship course is particularly fine, demanding a long straight drive to a plateau, from the edge of which you look over the clubhouse and down to a green guarded by two mature trees and a pond. Players of this hole will find it difficult to overcome a lack of confidence feeling at the prospect of hitting a 4-6 iron straight and true................

In all likelihood you will be amazed by the clubhouse. I have lost count of the times I have despaired over the average Briton's conception of what constitutes a clubhouse - the acceptance of all manner of inconveniences and low standards.

43

But Hill Valley is much more like it; much more like the American or continental patterns, with huge locker rooms. An incorporated professional's shop, a members only bar, two function rooms with one for Societies only and restaurant facilities that should put most club stewards to shame...............

With ambitious sporting and entertainment plans for the clubhouse Albert Minshall and Les Welch now have charge of one of the most exciting golf developments, not just in the Midlands but in Great Britain. Twenty seven holes, 18 of them championship standard and in addition to all the facilities they have John Anderson as club professional assisted by David Parry from Llangollen; David Vaughan the Welsh International and Tony Minshall are the tournament professionals and Ian Woosnam from Llanymynech is the Welsh Boys Captain. With weekday green fees at £2.76 and weekend green fees at £3.24 there can be few better bargains about. Something has stirred in Shropshire and the result should be a lesson to us all."

Peter Alliss and Les Welch.

1975 Press Day with Tony Parsonage third from right.

Peter Alliss and Albert.

Les Welch and Albert.

Some of the Press and Les Welch.

Bob Davies, reporter, Shropshire Star 1975

Dave Thomas and Les Welch

David Thomas, Beryl, Albert and Henry Longhurst at the opening

Hill Valley Golf and Country Club opens

THE sports and social life of Whitchurch is to be considerably brighter with the opening of the Hill Valley Golf and Country Club there last month.

The occasion was celebrated with a dinner for the chief guests and a buffet meal for the remainder of the 300 people who were invited to the official opening of the club house by Harry Longhurst, golfing journalist and author, Dave Thomas.

The night saw the fulfillment of an ambition of Mr. A. R. Minshull, of Wem, chairman of the project, and fellow businessmen. They are enthusiastic golfers themselves but in addition they believed the need for a first class golf course could be combined with other sports and social facilities of a high standard.

The result is a championship length 18-hole course and a 9-hole golf course on a site that 12 months ago was open farmland. The courses are overlooked by an attractive club house set in landscaped gardens. This boasts luxurious changing rooms and members bar and a professionals shop.

The building includes a restaurant seating 100, visitors bars and a dance floor. Mr. Minshull's wife is the club secretary and his son, Tony, is one of the team of professionals who will be working there.

Tournament professional is David Vaughan. John Anderson from Shrewsbury Golf Club is the club professional, assisted by David Parry from Llangollen. Ian Woosnam from Llanymynech, is the Welsh Boys Captain. The Midland Open Tournament will be held there this summer.

Club membership is going well with only a few vacancies for men golfers. Social members are welcome at the country club. They can relax in comfortable surroundings and enjoy the facilities of restaurant and bars.

On Wednesdays, Fridays and there will be regular cabaret is dancing to the resident gro

The next phase of the comp 50-bedroom luxury hotel, s minton courts and a swimm main function hall to seat 7

Mr. L. Welch, managing director, and Mrs.

Mr. G. Fox, president of the club, Mrs. Fox, Mr. A. W. Hiles, and Mrs. Margaret Hiles, Ladies Captain.

. A. J. Minshull, the chairman, with Mr. Henry Longhurst.

Mrs. Thomas, Mr. Dave Thomas, and Mrs. Minshull.

Former Ryder Cup star, Peter Allis (left), seen chatting with directors Albert Minshall and Les Welch, was full of praise for Hill Valley Golf Club at a club dinner last night. "Facilities here are second to none and there is not a clubhouse in the British Isles to compare with this. I don't think it will be long before you see one of the major professional events here," he told members.

Cuttings from the local press

THE OPENING OF HILL VALLEY GOLF COURSE
Press report
"Champagne start for Hill Valley"

"Saturday 29th June saw the official opening of a magnificent and challenging 18-hole championship course at the Hill Valley Golf and Country Club - the first phase of a £1 million plus project which must surely qualify as the most ambitious private development ever undertaken in Shropshire."

Peter Alliss, Malcolm Gregson and young caddy Ian Woosnam.

Over 4000 people came to watch the £250 a side challenge match to launch the new course. Peter Alliss, with Ian Woosnam as his caddy and another ex Ryder Cup star, Malcolm Gregson, just got the better of John Anderson and Tony Minshall in the exhibition round.

Press:

"Allis and Gregson finished one up over the 18 holes. They took an early lead and went 3 up at the par 5, 7th hole where Allis got an eagle. The club professionals began to play some fine golf to pull back the former Ryder Cup pair's lead to one up at the 12th and were unlucky not to level at the last six holes. At the 14th for instance Minshall just failed to sink a short putt and Anderson suffered a similar fate at the 16th."

Peter Alliss thanked his caddy Ian and gave him a wrapped Dunlop 65 ball. Then, after the match many people watched the half hour golf clinic conducted by Peter Alliss where he demonstrated and explained some basic and as well as some more advanced techniques of golf.

The press report concluded that, "The unanimous verdict was that the new course fulfilled all expectations and it will go down as a day to remember at Hill Valley, one that must have been amply rewarding to Mr. Albert Minshall, the chairman and the man behind the development. Mr. Wilf Birch, in welcoming the public on behalf of the club, paid tribute to Albert for his drive and initiative and Mr. Les Welch, his partner, for making it all possible."

Today, 'Hill Valley' Golf course is a name recognised and talked about by golfers all over the world.

THE OPENING OF THE CLUB HOUSE

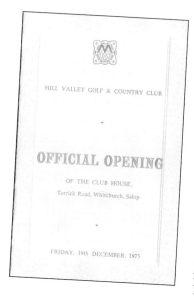

The Club House was officially opened with an inaugural dinner on December 19th 1975. The BBC commentator and author Henry Longhurst and Michael McDonnell from the Daily Mail were the guests of honour and both men gave excellent after dinner speeches. Dave Thomas was a guest of honour but unfortunately Peter Alliss was unable to attend the opening due to convalescence after an operation.

Mr. Henry Longhurst said that Hill Valley was part of the new explosion of golf that was bringing happiness, pleasure and delight to millions of people.

"May it give enormous happiness to enormous numbers of people so long as it lasts and may that be a very long time."

Mr. McDonnell replying on behalf of the guests spoke about Albert and Les.

Toast List

TOASTMASTER — THE CAPTAIN — J. DAVIES	
GRACE	
H.M. THE QUEEN — THE PRESIDENT — L. G. FOX	
THE HILL VALLEY GOLF & COUNTRY CLUB — PETER ALLISS	
GUESTS — A. J. MINSHALL	
REPLY — M. McCONNELL	

Menu

TEE OFF	7.30 P.M.
DRIVER	MELON AU COGNAC A LA BERYL
BRASSIE	LES CONSOMME MIMOSA
SPOON	SOLE ALBERT
MASHIE	TOURNEDOS A LA ALLISS VERT PRE POMMES PARISIAN CHOUFLEUR FRITOT
NIBLICK	OMELETE SURPRISE THOMAS
PUTTER	COFFEE & PETITE FOURS
CARRIAGES	1.30 A.M.

"They are a splendid partnership who have gone for the best and in my opinion have got it. They have set the standard and the course and the clubhouse are a true reward for their vision and ability."

The Shropshire Star reported the evening's events on December 20th 1975 under the headlines 'Hill Valley praised on opening night' and Albert said, "It's a night I shall never forget."

The seeds of an idea, sown in 1966, to own and build something that he had developed great passion for, had come to fruition by 1975 and he had also achieved a great union in combining his love for the game of golf, his business and his family. Beryl had had five children in the late 1950's and early 1960's: Tony, Carol, Louise, Wendy and Andrew. His family was complete. He introduced his children to golf at Hawkstone to include them in his sporting passion and it was then the part purchase of Hawkstone Park in 1967* that included the sport into his business. By 1973, having built his own golf course at Hill Valley, he had successfully completed the merging of these three cornerstones of his life.

Now, his whole family moved to a house on the Hill Valley land. Tony, his eldest son, was already playing excellent golf and preparing to turn professional. Any interest or talent the other children might develop in golf could be nurtured right there, along with the business, at home.

* Peter Alliss won over thirty titles including The Spanish Open twice in 1956 and 1958, The Italian Open in 1958, The Portugese Open in 1958 and The Brazilian Open in 1961. He won the Vardon Open as the leading money winner in 1964-1966.

* David Thomas was a prolific winner including The Belgium Open in 1955, The Dutch Open in 1958 and The French Open in 1959. He had memorable performances in The Open Championship where he finished as runner up on two occasions. Once in 1958 where he lost a play off to Peter Thomson and again in 1966 just losing to Jack Nicklaus.

* The syndicate sold Hawkstone Park in 1988.

Jeremiah 29:11

"For I know the plans I have for you," declares the Lord, " plans to prosper you and not to harm you, plans to give you hope and a future"

Monday-Friday (inc. Bank Holidays) £7.50
Weekend £11.00

Hill Valley Golf & Country Club

A delightful test of golf, ideally suited to the club and scratch golfer alike. The course, cleverly designed by International TV and golfing stars Peter Alliss and Dave Thomas, has fairways that thread their challenging way through the exciting 160 acres of Hill Valley's trees, lakes and picturesque streams to American style holding greens trapped by sand and water. The modern clubhouse, overlooking the 18th green, has a new sportsman's restaurant ideally suited for society catering — bar facilities available. Breakfast, bar snacks and full evening meals available throughout each day. Their is also two squash courts, billiards room with two tables, saunas and tennis courts.

Golf Director
and
Resident Professional:

TONY MINSHALL
Great Britain & Ireland PGA Cup
Team Player 1980 and 1982

For personal or group tuition and golf clinics (including indoor facilities, video TV recording, etc.) on a residential or daily basis, please contact the Professional Shop for an appointment.

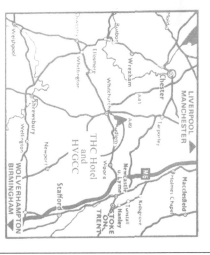

1) OF ONE THE FINEST INDOOR GOLF SCHOOL IN EUROPE

2) PERSONAL OR GROUP TUITION.

3) MAKE AND KEEP YOUR OWN VIDEO FILM.

4) COMPANY DAYS, USE A VIDEO AND ENJOY A GOLF CLINIC

TEL: (0948) 3584

JOHN GARNER
SCHOOL OF GOLF

RYDER CUP PLAYER
MATCHPLAY CHAMPION
IRISH NATIONAL COACH

JOHN GARNER SYSTEM

The inner pages of an early Hill Valley brochure

Hill Valley Golf and Country Club

— one of the most exciting new golf and entertainment complexes in the Midlands

Peter Alliss and Dave Thomas have designed Hill Valley's 18-hole championship golf course to the highest possible standards, presenting an exciting challenge to all golfers. The course, which has one of the finest finishing holes in the country, must surely be destined to become the venue for many major professional tournaments.

The adjoining 9-hole golf course provides the ideal venue for the beginner or the not so serious golfer.

The development at Hill Valley is being phased to eventually provide squash, tennis and badminton courts, and finally a 50 bedroomed modern hotel will complete the complex.

The modern, spacious club house accommodates four bars, billiards and table tennis room, professional's shop, golf practice room, dining room for over 100, entertainments and functions room, as well as the normal club house facilities. The restaurant opens at 8 a.m. and serves not only snacks but a full meal service until late evening. On at least three evenings per week disco and other types of cabaret and entertainment are provided at Hill Valley:

Wednesdays:	Terrick Suite	The Tennessee Stud Country Music Club
	Eagle Bar	Weekly Discotheque
Fridays:	Eagle Bar	Discotheque
Saturdays:	Terrick Suite	Valley Variety Club (cabaret from 8.30–12.30)
	Eagle Bar	Discotheque
Sundays:		Relaxing Sounds of Lance Pond at the Organ

We can offer full Breakfast, Lunch and Dinner Menus – for golf parties, private or firm parties, weddings or any type of function or entertainment. Please enquire at Reception or Telephone Peter Condliffe at 0948 3584.

TARIFF

Green Fees — 18 hole course

September 30th, 1976 to March 31st, 1977:

Weekdays and Weekends	... ...	£2.16 per day

April 1st, 1977 to September 30th, 1977:

Weekdays	... ...	£2.16 per day
Weekends and Bank Holidays	... ...	£3.24 per day

Typical Golfers' Party Menu

Arrival	Coffee and Biscuits	... ...	16p
Lunch	Soup and Sandwiches	... ...	65p
	Soup and Golfer's Platter	... ...	£1.15
Dinner	Three-course Meal	... ...	£2.00

SOCIETIES AND VISITORS ARE ALWAYS WELCOME AT
HILL VALLEY GOLF & COUNTRY CLUB
For details contact Les Welch @ 0948 3584

The inner pages of an early Hill Valley brochure

PART TWO

9th Tee:

The Golf Club at Hill Valley 1975 - 2006

9th Hole - Par 4 - 370 yards

A ninety degree dogleg left with out of bounds following the hole down the left hand side the more aggressive player will attack the corner leaving a short iron in to the green, mere mortals will play straight at the marker hitting a mid iron into the green defended by bunkers on both sides.

"There must always be plenty of tea and good sandwiches."

Albert

1. The Mens', The Ladies', The Seniors', The Juniors'.

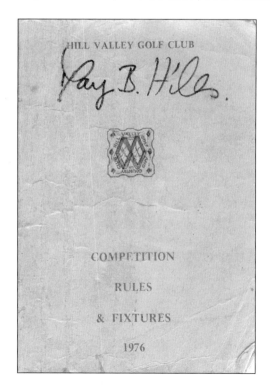

The first trophy presentation evening at the Hill valley Golf Course - 1975

*Presidents and captains of Hill Valley celebrate the 10th
anniversary of the golf course in 1985*

Trophy presentation time at Hill Valley 1975

THE MENS' SECTION

Bob Walker, a founder member, was Membership Hon. Secretary for Men's and Juniors at Hill Valley 1977-1992 and general secretary for the Golf Club for Albert from 1980-1998.

The subs for the first July to December 1975 were £70 and all applications for membership were approved. Duncan Shepard was the first member of the new golf club to come and play. Albert wouldn't take any money off him and waived his green fee.

Warrington Golf Classic 1992

Brian Hockenhull (left) and members

Harry Carr, Tony Minshall, Albert Minshall and John Hanlon

Anthony Smith, 1995 (Hill Valley President 2006/07)
England Amateur Senior International

Rob Ashbrook, Michael Welch, Carl Cieielski, John Williams,
Duncan Hall and Andrew Hall - Hargrove Trophy winners

Handicap League Winners

Hill Valley Trophy presentation. Robert Williams, Eddie Peate, Stan Chesters, Albert Minshall, Wilf Lyman, Bob Walker, Babs Jones and Brian Hockenhull, President

George Ashworth - 1977

Tony Minshall, Maurice Reeves, Albert and Peter Condliff

1977 Pro Am. Alan Molyneux, Stan Chester, Graham Steel and Lenny Chester

Mr Terry Squires, pro, Stan Chester, Gerald Smith and Kevin Smith

THE LADIES SECTION

"You can't run a golf club without a good ladies' section and that's what we've always had."

Albert

"I always believed that the ladies had as much right on a golf course as men. We've got a good ladies' section at Hill Valley and it's always been good and as long as I'm here I'll always try to help the ladies with whatever tournament they want and to enjoy their golf."

MARGARET HILES

When the course opened in 1975 Albert asked Margaret Hiles to run the ladies' section which she did until the club became officially affiliated to The Shropshire and Herefordshire Union and also the Ladies' Golf Union (LGU) on January 1st 1976. Margaret then became the first Lady Captain.

The first ladies' open was held in July 1976 with players from 21 clubs and 5 counties.

First ladies' annual dinner: Speaker and prizes presented by Carol Comboy OBE, First Lady Captain of England and Great Britain Ladies' Golf Team.

In November 2006 Margaret Hiles was awarded an Honorary Life Membership at Hill Valley Golf Club for all her hard work and excellent fundraising through the years.

Ladies Golf Club dinner

The Hill Valley Ladies Golf Club, Whitchurch, held their first annual dinner at the Hill Valley Golf Club.

Mrs Mary Pickering, Mrs Babs Jones.

Mrs Emma Cawkwell, Mrs Dorothy Perry, Mrs Ann Jackson, Mrs Sheila Johnson, Mrs Margaret Barnett, Mrs Hazel Jones, Mrs Chris Ellson, Mrs Rose Welch.

Mrs Kathleen Carr, Mrs Eileen Evans, Mrs Mary Wise, Mrs Janet Bishop.

Mrs Stella Dodd, Mrs Elma Brown, Mrs Dorothy Goodwin.

Mrs Dorothy Rowland, Mrs Margaret Preston, Mrs Gladys Dodd.

Mrs Betty Hollins, Mrs Freda Boughey, Mrs Doreen Osbourne.

Mrs Beryl Minshall, Mrs Olga Thomasson, Miss Carol Minshall, Miss Dawn Thomasson.

Pictures: Richard Brock

Ladies Golf Dinner - 1976

Debut year success for Hill Valley

More than 160 people attended Hill Valley Golf Club's first annual dinner and presentation.

Guest speaker was Mr Hubert Smith, who congratulated the club on the success it has had during its first year and the members who had worked so hard to achieve this.

Trophies were presented by club captain, Mr John Davies with the toast to the club being made by the president, Mr Geoff Fox.

In the ladies' section, captain, Mrs Margaret Hiles was presented with the Stella Dodd Rose Bowl and the Harry Carr Cup. The Menwal Designs Cup went to Mrs Margaret Hollins and Mrs Beryl Minshall.

Mrs Barbara Jones was presented with the Bill Smith Cup and the president's prize (ladies). Mrs Mary Edwards took the Ladies' Captain's Prize.

The Margaret Hiles Brooch awarded to the winner of the ladies' knock-out competition went to Mrs Margaret Hollins.

In the men's section, the Club Championship Trophy went to Mr Ian Woosnam with the N. H. and J. Peate Cup being won jointly by Mr Ron White and Mr Tony Ciesielski.

The Wem Services Veterans' Cup was presented to Mr Oscar Williams with the W. H. Smith Cup going to Dr Mike Jones. Mr Don Armstrong and Mr Stuart Wood were joint winners of the S. Chesters Cup.

Winners of the Herald Rose Bowl were Mr George Ashworth and Mr John Arthan with Mr Ian Woosnam winning the Peter Allis Trophy and Dr Mike Jones, the Easter Cup.

In the mixed section, Mrs Margaret Hiles, together with Mr Ron White were presented with the Frank and Mary Johnson Cup with the Bateman Perpetual Trophy going to Mrs Margaret Barnett and Mr John Wood.

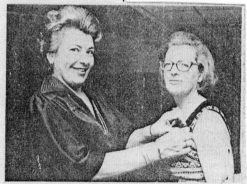

Mrs Hiles (left) presenting her brooch award to Mrs Margaret Hollins.

1976

68

Some of the members and guests at the first ladies annual prize-giving evening.

Seen at the top of the table at the ladies annual prize-giving are left Carol Comboy with Mrs Margaret Hilles, team captain.

Golf club honours work of fundraiser

IN THE SWING: Margaret Hiles, centre, is awarded honorary life membership of Hill Valley Golf Club by golf co-ordinator Kelly Lowe and golf manager Jamie Minshall.
JK081106golfclub-001

CATCHING UP: Whitchurch residents Harold Wilde, Doreen Povey, June Groom, Elaine and Ron Smith chat to senior tourism assistant Sandra Marsh at Whitchurch Heritage Centre's monthly coffee morning. vc011106coffee

A COMMUNITY fundraiser from Whitchurch is on the fairway to heaven after receiving an award for her support.

Hill Valley Golf Club has awarded honorary life membership to Margaret Hiles, chairwoman of Whitchurch Hospital's League of Friends.

Mrs Hiles was the club's first lady captain in 1976, and helped homegrown talent Ian Woosnam, the club's junior captain at the time, reach the circuit.

In 1993 she was the first lady president at Hawkstone Park Golf Club, where she is currently an honorary member.

Golf co-ordinator Kelly Lowe, daughter of Tony Minshall, said: 'Mrs Hiles has done a lot for the club. She's currently helping a talented 19-year-old, who is on a handicap of one, get sponsorship in the same way she helped Ian.

'We see the hard work she puts in to fundraising as she often holds events here, and we'd like to give her something in return.'

Although Mrs Hiles is currently suffering a shoulder injury, she is looking forward to making the most of her membership as soon as possible.

'It was such a shock when they told me,' she said. 'I've been an honorary member for many years but to be given it for life is really special.'

Lady captain Margaret Hiles on a golf day out with friends.

THE SENIORS

There has always been an active senior section at Hill Valley. They play their own fixtures and tournaments and arrange their own events such as their Christmas party.

Hill Valley has been as one senior member reflected, 'It's not just the buildings and not even all the golf, it's the people here who have made it such a comfortable and enjoyable place to be.'

Albert, Kenny McClellan and David Aldridge on the completion of the Leisure Centre at Hill Valley

1976. Ian Woosnam Club Champion.
Stuart Wood Junior Champion.

THE JUNIORS

Ian Woosnam was the first Junior Captain at Hill valley and won the first club championship at Hill Valley in 1976 while still only a junior member.

John Williams, a founder member at the age of thirteen was the first junior at Hill Valley to represent the county. Jon Safhil, a fellow junior member, joined him.

John has good memories of those early days playing golf at Hill Valley. Albert would come and play a few holes with the juniors encouraging them and telling them to help themselves to a different driver or putter from the pro shop if he felt it would help their game. Tony Minshall and Ian Woosnam would hold free coaching sessions for all the juniors on Saturday mornings. Ron White and Bill Smith were responsible for organising the junior events. The juniors were a thriving and lively part of the golf club.

John Williams remembers one occasion when Albert took him and John Safhill to a junior tournament at Shifnall. They were travelling in Albert's Rolls Royce and just south of Whitchurch when Albert saw a man thumbing a lift on the side of the road. He was poorly dressed and unkempt but Albert asked him where he would like to go.

The man replied that he was trying to visit his son who was incarcerated at Stoke Heath Remand Centre. Albert went out of his way to give the man a lift all the way to the prison gates in his Rolls Royce and gave the man a five pound note so that he could get home.

John Williams with early Junior Members.

John Anderson is presented with an award from Ron White junior section organiser and Bill Smith junior president.

Mrs J Bishop is seen holding the junior Stapleford Cup with some of the young competitors at Hill Valley.

Club pro John Anderson presents John Williams with his trophy after he won the annual junior competition at Hill Valley.

Pslams 34:18

The Lord is close to the broken hearted and saves those who are crushed in spirit.

Pslams 49:20

A man who has riches without understanding, is like the beasts that perish.

10th Tee:

The Professionals at Hill Valley

10th Hole - Par 4 - 392 yards

The tee shot here requires you to thread the ball safely between the oak tree on the right and willow tree on the left. The fairway falls away in front of you in to a small valley. The second shot will just require a short iron into a generous green with bunkers either side.

"Albert brings out the best in people."

Tony Parsonage

THE PROFESSIONALS 1975-2006

John Anderson
Kevin Valentine
Neil Humphries
David Hislop 2003-2006
Clive Burgess 1999-2004, 2006 to present.
Rob Ashbrook 1995-2000
John Garner
Shaun Walsh 1993-1999
Rainer Jarman 1993-1999
Peter Baker 2004-2005 Attached Euro Tour pro.
Steve Carter Attached playing pro 2000-2006
Jon Lomas Attached Euro Tour pro.
Phil Seed Attached Euro Tour pro.
John Mashego Attached seniors Tour Professional

TONY MINSHALL

Tony Minshall, Albert's eldest son, began caddying for his father at the age of seven. Then, still as a young boy he began to play golf with the talent and promise of a future champion. He was a junior member at Hawkstone Park and his talent was nurtured playing alongside some other excellent players, including his peer Sandy Lyle whose father, Alex Lyle, was the long established professional at Hawkstone through those years. Alex taught Tony in those early years and Tony's handicap reduced to 4, the required number to turn professional in 1972.

Tony and Sir Henry Cotton in 1972, Pennina, Portugal.

In 1972, at the age of fifteen, Tony played in the county trials, The Jeffrey Clee Salver and the Shropshire and Herefordshire Amateur Championship. Albert also played in the County Championship at Oswestry and together they both qualified for The Shropshire Open Championship at Lilleshall Hall. Tony played with Gwilliam Hardiman in that event as an Amateur and he scored 79+77.

At the end of that season and with a handicap now in low single figures the decision was made that he should turn professional. It was 1972, the same year that Albert bought the land to build Hill Valley.

Sir Henry Cotton.

Albert sent Tony to a succession of instructors to progress his professional playing career. He spent some time with Patrick Tallack at Moor Park and attended training sessions with John Jacobs at North Shore in Blackpool. Sir Henry Cotton at Pennina also tutored him and Tony, like many good players, benefited well from the advice given to him by one of the greatest golfing champions in Britain but someone who had also done so much to help the development of golf in his own country. John Anderson who coached Tony in Shrewsbury played the Hill Valley opening game on 29th June 1975. He went on to become the Hill Valley's first professional.

Tony became attached to Lilleshall Golf Club under Gwilliam Hardiman and from there began his attempt to break into the P.G.A. European tournament circuit. There was no European tour, as it is known today. The PGA controlled all the professional events in the UK and Ireland and also administered open championships on the continent. In order to compete in the continental Open Championships a professional player also had to pre-qualify a few days before the event began. In 1973, aged just sixteen Tony qualified and played his first full professional year. He competed in four continental events, The French, The Dutch, The Swiss Opens and the first Scandinavian Enterprises Open in Stockholm.

Tony Minshall and Jamie Minshall.

Mad Dogs And Englishmen

At the age of 16, Albert sent Tony to compete in a golf tour in Nigeria. At that time Tony had never been further than Shrewsbury, his local market town, in his life. When he boarded the plane at Gatwick airport he thought the journey would be along the runway, overland all the way. He got a shock as they lifted into the air. When the doors of the plane were opened in Nigeria, Tony and his friend Andy Griffiths were still wearing their greatcoats suitable for a cold British winter. They nearly passed out with the heat. They took £100 each with them for their eight-week tour. After paying their caddies and general daily expenses they returned with £60 such was the kindness and generosity of the golf tour hosts in Nigeria. Tony recalls his and Andy's dedication to their game and drive for success. Every day of the tour they would go out and practice hitting balls for hours in the heat and under the fierce midday sun. A lifelong friendship with Andy Griffiths was cemented.

In 1974 Tony competed again in the Shropshire Open at The Wrekin. After rounds of 71+67 he finished in runner up position but leading professional behind Sandy Lyle.

Tony went on to become very closely involved with the development of his father's project, Hill Valley.

In 1984 Tony retired from the pro circuit.

"I wish I could have stuck at it. I enjoyed my career and met a lot of good people. I know I could have gone to the top. I had the talent and the dedication to the game but I didn't like travelling and I couldn't see a way forward to resolve that."

Albert, reflecting on what a good teacher Alex Lyle was to Tony, wonders if he himself made a mistake helping Tony too much, for example, sending Tony to Nigeria for eight weeks at such a young age. He regrets that he only recognized much later that Tony did not like the world travel necessary in the golfing world and was happier playing closer to home.

Tony however counters this by saying, "It was not Dad's fault. It was other things. I had a wife and young family. I couldn't have a better dad if I had gone all around the world looking for one. He's always been straight and fair and always been there for me. As has my mother. Both of them. Sending me to Africa was the best thing he did. It was a great life experience. I learned how to treat people. I wouldn't change anything."

When Tony was young he learnt bricklaying and building jobs, building manholes, windowsills, footings, "perhaps I should have stuck at that, I was doing very well!"

Tony played the Pro am circuit for a while, Albert had sunk all his money into Hill Valley and he ran the shop and helped run the business.

He played for GB & Ireland in the Johnny Walker PGA cup teams in 1980 in America on a golf course in Olkahoma at Oak Tree Golf Course resort and again at Muirfield in 1983. Tony was Shropshire open champion six times (79,80,82,83,84 and again in 1997 coming out of retirement) Northern Open (now known as The Challenge Tour) In the European Tour, 9th was Tony's best finish. He also won all of the Midland PGA titles and the Northern Open in 1982 at Cruden Bay.

Tony Minshall.

ANDREW MINSHALL

Andrew was three years old when Albert bought the land that was to become Hill Valley so he grew up in a home overlooking the developing golf course. He played rugby at school but left at fifteen to play golf. He played as an amateur for two years, working on building renovations at Hill Valley in the mornings and then playing golf in the afternoons. Albert arranged for him to spend six weeks in the USA under the tutorship of David Clay. There were no golf academies in Great Britain at the time, so when he flew home he planned to return to America for more coaching. However, he broke his arm on the day that he landed back in the UK and he never did return to train in the USA. Perhaps a missed opportunity but at the age of seventeen, he turned professional at Hill Valley. He played in the European Challenge Tour and many regional tournaments with reasonably good results.

His golfing career came to an abrupt end when at the age of only twenty-one, a childhood injury to his back resurfaced under the physical pressure of playing golf so constantly and at such a high level. His spinal discs were so damaged that he was told he wouldn't even walk let alone play golf again. They were reluctant to operate as there was a 70% chance of paralysis so after a long stay in hospital he came home to Hill Valley to work on the golf course with the green keepers. He attended Reese Heath College to learn more about golf courses and green keeping.

Andrew didn't pick up a golf club for nearly three years. After the initial shock at the sudden ending of his career as a professional golfer and his subsequent long recovery, he found he adjusted well to his new life and was happy in his new career on the course but not playing. On reflection he says, "I didn't miss it at all and it was the happiest three years of my life."

It was a founder member, Anthony Smith, who one day at Hill Valley, asked Andrew if he would play as an amateur in a county match with the second team as they were short of players. He did so and went straight into playing with the first team, winning The County Match in 1999. Once he had begun to play again he found he played more and more frequently and even started competing in pro events as an amateur, becoming exempt from qualifying in 1994. He entered the Pro MasterCard Tour in 2000 and again in 2001. This tournament became the Euro Pro Tour from 2002. In June 2004 Andrew went to Montenegro for a day to investigate possibilities in golf course development and he quickly realised there was a new opportunity there for him to pursue. That summer he played in the 2004 Euro Pro Tournament. As he finished his last hole in the competition he said, "That's it, I'm finished playing."

'You can't pack it in,' my mates said,' you won't be able to do it.' Well, I have done it and I don't miss it. As much fun as it is playing golf every week, it's also hard work. All the travelling and you have no real family life. It's not just what you're doing on the golf course, the going out to play, it's also all the time spent practicing. It's a selfish game but it pays the bills. So many golf players are either divorced or they've given up playing.

Will I ever play again? No chance. My back was never really brilliant through those years; it was never going to be perfect so I couldn't give the game what it needs to be given. I did it for Dad and he was happy that I was playing again. It looked good for the club and the members were always interested. I was very fortunate, there are a lot worse jobs. But I couldn't go on and anyway I was too old and too broken down but I did as well as I could under the circumstances. I'm happy now developing courses and working on them but I'll never play competition golf again."

IAN WOOSNAM (b1958)

Ian was Junior Captain at Hill Valley for two years from 1975-1976. He worked behind the bar and on the door for the Disco's at Hill Valley and also on the course, planting many of the trees, especially all those on the right of the third fairway.

Albert recalls that Ian was a 'good lad', who never got into any trouble, despite some fiery young lads around him on some evenings. In the afternoons he would go out onto the golf course and practice with a will to succeed in his chosen game. What was noted about Ian at Hill Valley and subsequently, was that he played in exactly the same manner when under pressure in a major tournament as when knocking about, whatever his score. That will to succeed along with such consistency of thought and such an early established swing are perhaps some of the marks of a great player.

Ian

My years at Hill Valley put me on the road to success. Without Albert and Tony's early help I wouldn't be where I am today. I might still be on the farm where I grew up. Albert was a calming influence and Tony looked after me well. We all worked hard, turning our hand to all sorts of jobs, throwing ourselves into whatever needed doing. I saw the first Hill Valley clubhouse being built and helped to plant some of those 40.000 trees. I was paid £10 a week, £5 for digs and £5 for food.

I was allowed to have a childhood. We were one big happy family. Albert let us be boys, be young lads, as long as we worked hard, he let us have fun and we did both. I remember being pulled into the office with the pro after too many pints one night in the clubhouse. But as long as we worked hard too we were allowed to get on with what we wanted to do and have a good time. There was a family atmosphere and without those times I wonder what I would have done. I have very good memories of my time at Hill Valley. Albert gave opportunities to us youngsters who were starting out in life. He gave me the valuable chance, which I hadn't had until then, to play golf in the afternoons and I had many hours of practice. That playing and practice time is critical to develop your game and in

Tony and Ian Woosnam at Hill Valley in 1989.

those days it was fairly unique for an assistant pro to play and practice in the afternoons. He used to say, 'If you work hard and practice hard success will come to you', and he also said, 'Never give up hope'.

I'd like to thank Albert and Tony for those two years and the opportunities they gave me at Hill Valley."

Albert:

"Ian came back and played at Hill Valley a few years ago and his swing was still the same. We might have offered him facilities in those early days and the course was tougher than it is now, but his swing is the same now as it was when he was sixteen, so we can't take credit for his achievements. It has been good to have an association with him over these years and we've remained friends."

THE IAN WOOSNAM CORNER

Ian Woosnam was attached to Hill Valley Golf and Country Club from 1975 when the Club was formally opened for Golf. He remained here until 1979 during which time he lived in what is today Bedroom 9. (commonly known as Woosie's room).

Ian was our first Club Champion in 1975 and also won the inaugural Peter Alliss Trophy in the same Year.

During his time at Hill Valley, Ian was employed in many areas of activity. He played a big part in planting many of the wonderful mature trees that surround the Courses today. He worked behind the Bar and frequently acted as a 'Bouncer' when the Club was a 'NITE SPOT'.

Eventually turning Professional, it was through the efforts of the Hill Valley Members, and in particular Mrs Margaret Hiles and Mr Bill Smith, that sufficient funds were made available to send Ian on his first foreign trip – a trip which proved to be the first step on an absolutely fabulous Professional Golfing Career.

We congratulate Ian on his achievements and we commemorate them by dedicating this corner of the Sportsman's Bar to the Memory's. We know that Hill Valley represents just a stepping stone in a marvellous career for the Great Man, and we hope there are many more fine successes yet to come.

May a little of Ian's magic rub off on those guests who stay in Room 9 (Woosie's Room).

Ian Woosnam's
FIRST STEPS TO STARDOM
Come along to
Bertie's Birthday Bonanza Party
on TUESDAY, 1st MARCH, 1977
at HILL VALLEY GOLF & COUNTRY CLUB
Food served at 9 p.m.   :   Licensed Bar 8 p.m.—1 a.m.
All proceeds will be given to Ian to help pay for his first professional Golf Tournament (£600)
Presentation of cheque to be made by Mrs. Margaret Hiles at 12 o'clock

Tickets : : : :   £2.00 each
Jackets and Ties please

Home, sweet home!

PLAYING on his home course at Hill Valley, Whitchurch, one of the club's professionals, 19-year-old Ian Woosnam, won the Shropshire and Herefordshire open golf championship on Wednesday last week.

After the two 18-rounds, Woosnam finished level on 151 with two amateurs, Basil Griffiths (Oswestry) and Bob Clemson (Shifnal), and the situation called for a sudden-death play-off in which Woosnam had a birdie four on the first extra hole — the 500 yards 16th. Griffiths and Clemson both missed their birdie putts.

This was Woosnam's first triumph in the tournament and he set the pace right from the start to finish the first round with a one-under-par 71, the only sub-par round of the day. But he almost ruined his chances by taking 80 second time round.

Last year's champion, Hawkstone Park's Anthony Smith, was again very much in contention and finished just a stroke behind the leading trio, on 152. Two strokes behind him, together three other competitors, was Hill Valley's Tony Minshall.

Leading scores were: 151 — Ian Woosnam (Hill Valley), R. Clemson (Shifnal), B. Griffiths (Oswestry); 152 — M. A. Smith (Hawkstone Park); 154 — Tony Minshall (Hill Valley), M. Moseley

■ Ian Woosnam, winner of the Shropshire and Herefordshire open golf championship at Hill Valley last week.

■ Tony Minshall (Shrewsbury) Minshall

Woosnam staying in amateur ranks

Woosnam takes Valley title

Former Shropshire champion Ian Woosnam has become club champion at Hill Valley.

The Welsh international shot rounds of 75 and 76 to won from Kurt Pluke, who scored 78 and 80.

August medal winner was Mr Grange with 37-22-59 with P. White runner-up on 31-19-72.

Other leading scores were: K. Valentine 92-19-73, J. Wood 95-22-73, I. Woosnam 75-1-74, R. B. Walker 98-24-74, B. Siertsema 88-14-74, J. Davies 88-14-74, J. B. Hughes 83-8-75.

In the women's section, winners of the Menval Design Foursomes Cup were M. Hollins and B. Minshall with A. Newman and H. . . . 49.

The Greensomes Cup was won by . . . les and M. Bewit . . . S. Dodd and Mc . . . with the August Med . . . won M. Pickering, with J. Dixon runner-up.

James Williams, who has played for the Shropshire second team, won the junior club championship at Shrewsbury, where he is junior captain.

He totalled 111—68 and 73—to won from Gareth Sambrook, who scored 77 and 78 for a total of 155.

Morning round winner with net 65 was I. Taylor and afternoon winner N. Pluto with 61. Pluto also won the 36-hole net with rounds of 66 and 61.

Kevin Road, who has only been playing golf for a few months, holed in one at the eighth.

Ian Woosnam

MICHAEL WELCH (b1989)
Attached Playing Professional until 2003

"He was one of the best young players I've ever seen. He could still get to the top. I first saw him play at 16 and he has played at Hill Valley for many years. At present he lives and plays at Hawkstone Park, he often comes up to Hill Valley now to catch up with all the lads. I still watch the results, I hope he goes onto win a tournament. He certainly should. He always had the belief. It wouldn't surprise me if he wins in the near future."

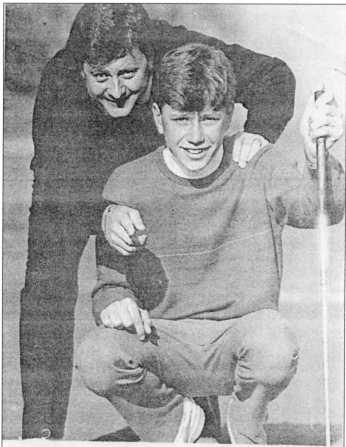

Young golfer of the year, Michael Welch of Hawkstone Park, receives some expert advice from golfing super star, Ian Woosman, who was at Patshull Park today holding a clinic. He gave the youngster a few tips on the putting green.

MATTHEW EDWARDS

One young player, Matthew Edwards, recently impressed Albert. His quiet and gentle manner and smart appearance was reminiscent of Sandy Lyle for Albert. At the age of fifteen, and a junior member of Hill Valley, Matthew decided he would like to pursue a golfing career. An opening was offered to him in the pro shop with the encouragement and possibility to play golf and develop his game as well as help with funding for entering tournaments, such as South Africa in January 2007.

"Without the Minshall family backing and being here at Hill Valley, I wouldn't have been able to develop my game and my career as I have done. I'm entering tournaments and aiming for where I want to be as a professional golfer."

Albert:

"There are so many distractions now but we try to encourage them, play with them, help them along and hand on a few tricks we've learnt over the years. Now we've learnt not to push too much too long. I say to the youngsters 'don't rush it', take tournaments as they come. Don't get there to quickly, pace yourself. Ian was 22-24 when he began to win his big tournaments so at 18 years old, he has plenty of time to gain the experience that is needed on the golf course. Develop your own mind and don't get there to early. There have been many talented players through Hill Valley but they decide sometimes to go other ways."

Proverbs 16:9

In his heart a man plans his course, but the Lord determines his steps.

11th Tee:

Tales From The Tees Around Hill Valley Golf Course

11th Hole - Par 4 - 390 yards

On the tee you can see the fairway in front of you but at driver distance there lies a hollow in the fairway, hit too far and play from there completely blind to the hole. Most players lay short with a fairway wood hitting a mid to short iron into the green, danger lies on the left hand side with a large bunker gathering wayward shots.

"Golf inspires good behaviour."

Tony Hateley

TALES FROM THE TEES

Early Days on the new Hill Valley Course

"I remember the very first days of the course nearing completion in the spring of 1975 before it was officially opened at the end of June. A group of us would play golf and then one member brought his tractor so we would all ride on this tractor all over the fairways jumping off to pick up all the remaining rocks and stones that were still in the way and throw them into the trailer. Then, as there was no clubhouse built yet, we would all jump back on and go to the nearest house where Peter Condliffe, the first manager, would cook us up the most wonderful bacon and eggs provided by Albert. A feast! Albert felt strongly that he always wanted his players to be able to get whatever refreshment they wanted when they wanted. 'A steak at eight in the morning if they want that', he would say. None of us who were there have ever forgotten Peter's breakfast fry ups for us. There was a good feeling of camaraderie and unity in a great new venture."

Margaret Hiles

Tales From The 1st Tee:

"Neil Humphries, the young assistant pro to Tony, rang me one morning, 'There are eight men on the 1st tee fighting about who is to go first,' he said. 'Things are getting very heated, you'd better come quickly'.

I hurried up there, collecting four cans of beer on my way. I gave one can each to the group of four lads who were smaller and quickly set the four larger men on their way first. It was a rare occurrence; most people are very well behaved on a golf course. Except for one other occasion. There's a pond on left of first fairway. A player was late arriving for his game and finding his place had been taken was so angry he picked up my trolley and threw it into the pond. Albert laughed his socks off.

Bob Walker

TALE FROM THE 5TH TEE:

In 1986, the 10th anniversary year for Hill Valley, Albert was playing in a mixed tournament with professional player, Maureen Madill. Bob Walker partnered Mary Done.

At the 5th Tee Maureen, who was playing her first round on the Hill Valley golf course asked Albert for some direction advice. Albert replied, "Do you see that tree over there, and then the branch to the left? Well there's a smaller branch just pointing down..."

"Just a minute," Maureen interrupted, "Exactly which leaf are you going to ask me to hit?"

TALES FROM THE 9TH TEE:

Old Cyril was sitting having a peaceful lunch one day taking his break from raking the bunkers, when a golf ball came flying through his window, landing smack into the butter in the butter dish. Cyril, calmly finished his lunch, carefully washed the ball and handed it back to Tony in the golf shop.

Stan Chester was playing the 9th hole one day when a crow flew down, picked up Stan's ball in his beak and flew away. Stan's fellow players watched as he ran down the fairway waving his club wildly and shouting ripe language at the disappearing bird. He was allowed to place another ball.

A similar event happened to Tony during a European Tournament. A cat wandered onto the course and playfully pushed Tony's ball off the green. Luckily for Tony, television cameras had recorded the cat's antics so officials were able to agree that Tony's ball be replaced. Twenty-five years later in 2005, a similar event happened to a golfer in another competition and Tony and his cat incident were referred to as precedent for allowing the ball to be replaced.

TALES FROM THE 12TH TEE:

Albert was driving a brand new Rolls Royce from the 12th green to the 12th tee. Bob Walker was beside him and they were listening intently to the news on the car radio about the attack on the Sir Galahad Naval Ship during the Falklands War. Suddenly the front end of the car disappeared sharply downwards. He had driven straight into the bunker. It took a mechanical digger and the help of several members to get the car out and safely back onto the road. The next day the bunker was filled in.

Albert was playing golf one day and arriving at the twelfth tee he saw a car, with a ladder strapped to the roof, coming towards him alongside the course. He asked the driver where he was going. The driver, who was with his son, explained that after hitting his ball into the rough he had become frustrated and thrown his club into the air in despair. It had landed near the top of an old oak tree and stuck there so he was returning to retrieve it.

Psalm 39 V6

Man is a mere phantom to and fro. He bustles about, but only in vain he heaps up wealth, not knowing who will get it.

Psalm 490 V10

For all can see that wise men die; the foolish and the senseless alike perish and leave their wealth to others.

12th Tee:

Celebrity Golf at Hill Valley

12th Hole - Par 4 - 355 yards

A blind tee shot over the top of the bank with trees tight either side. The sensible play is to lay up short of the two oak trees, the green is set slightly elevated from the fairway with two bunkers at the back but fall short to the left and the chip shot up to the green is tough.

TONY HATELEY/NORMAN WISDOM

SPARKS - CHARITY GOLF

"I've played four or five celebrity golf games a year with Albert for 30 years. To have known him and been associated with him is an honour. I love the man to bits."

Tony Hateley

Sparks Isle of Man. The first get together in 1970.
Tony Hateley, Cyril Forrester, Norman Wisdom and Albert.

Sparks reunion, Tony Hateley, Norman Wisdom, Albert. 2006.

Tony West, Frank Carson and Albert at Hill Valley.

COLIN YOUNG

World Record at Hill Valley 1999

Colin Young, a presenter for BBC Radio Shropshire, decided to try and break the world record for the greatest number of holes played in a week. Colin had set a record of 1260 in 1988. An American man broke this record and set a new world record completing 1702 holes in a week in 1998.

Colin chose the Hill Valley course to try to break this world record for several reasons. He had been invited to play at Hill Valley several times as a celebrity so he knew the course and he needed a hotel within the grounds. Most importantly he had always felt very welcome and well looked after every visit he had made. Colin's father had also played golf with Albert a few times and found their hospitality kind and generous. He knew he would need good support from the hosts to enable him to give it his best shot at breaking the record. Colin's bid was in aid of 'The Sky's the Limit' County Air Ambulance Appeal.

He knew his attempt was going to be tough, made even more so by recent major knee surgery.

The record attempt began at 12.00 noon on Monday 2nd August and was to finish at 12.00 noon on Monday 9th August. The course was open for business as usual and Colin completed eight rounds on that first afternoon weaving his way as quickly as he could through other players.

Hill Valley organised sponsoring for Colin and had hundreds of balls made for him. He was up each morning ready to start hitting balls as soon as the visibility allowed him, which was around 4.30am. He then continued until the light faded at around 9.30pm. He finally got to bed around 11pm for a short night's rest before starting all over again.

Hill Valley played a great part keeping Colin very well fed and watered, caddying and driving the buggy around for him working hard to make his record attempt as smooth and attainable as possible for him. Tony Minshall was up at 4.00am a few times to drive the buggy and even his 14-year-old daughter, Kelly, drove a few times. She won the award for the fastest buggy driver with a record of 53 minutes for a round. Albert also drove and tried to relieve any sense of monotony or fatigue for Colin by chatting about plans for improvement to the complex, but Colin said later his focus was so entirely on what he was trying to do that he found it increasingly hard to take anything else in except nourishment. In fact his determination increased when on the fifth day he suddenly realised that the world record was in sight but it was also the day when all the physical exertion of the week, combined with hot weather and so much time in the sun, culminated in the possibility of severe dehydration. Tony recognised the signs and loaded up the buggy with buckets of ice and wet towels and cases of cold water to stave off any emergency or halt in the record attempt. It was this tremendous support along with great encouragements Colin received all week from all the other players on the course that sustained Colin through his moments of great fatigue.

The Sunday, however, was to prove the hardest day of them all. Four hours of torrential rain flooded the greens and Colin couldn't get the balls into the holes. All the other players had left the waterlogged course. Colin, the only player still out there, exhausted and soaked, knew that this, at almost the eleventh hour, would be the end for his attempt if he gave in and he was so close. As the thunder crashed and lightening sparked above him he was advised, 'Well, it's at your own risk' but left to continue. The storm passed, the greens cleared quickly and at last he was through to the final Monday morning. Radio stations rang through for progress reports and TV cameras arrived to watch him play his final rounds. With 45 minutes to go and by one hole he broke the world record. He continued playing three more holes and was joined in play by Tony Minshall, Graeme Bagnall, Clive Burgess and Sarah White form Central TV. There were great celebrations on the 18th green and his grand total was 1706 holes in the time allowed. His forms were all verified and countersigned. He had broken the world record with a comfortable four-hole margin.

Colin played 8500 shots, travelled around 300 miles in the buggy and raised £4500 for the Air Ambulance appeal. It had been a great week for Colin and he had achieved a new world record with tremendous support from Hill Valley.

Apart from the celebrity golf games events Albert also encouraged other celebrity charity events at Hill Valley. Ken Dodd brought a theatre performance to Hill Valley in 1979. It was still relatively early days for Hill Valley and Ken Dodd opened the show with the line, "This is the first time I've ever performed in a shed."

Roger Taylor, Wimbledon winner opened the newly surfaced and refurbished tennis courts at the Terrick Hotel in 1980.

A ticklish moment

Comedian Ken Dodd, armed with his famous tickling stick, enjoys a joke on a visit to Whitchurch last week. On the receiving end are Albert Minshall (right) a proprietor of Hill Valley Golf and Country Club, where Ken appeared, and five times world snooker champion Ray Reardon of Market Drayton.

20 THE WHITCHURCH HERALD, WEDNESDAY, MAY 8, 198?

Soapers and jokers do the rounds

LUCKILY Frank Carson is only joking and 12-year-old Michael Welsh does

Mrs Faldo's letter to Stan Chester after the Midland Pro Tournament.

*Brian Peake, Neville Metcalf, Nick Faldo and Stan Chester.
Midlands open at Hill Valley, 1970's.*

Sarah Roache, William Roache (Coronation Street) and Albert.

Willy Morgan, Manchester United and Scotland Footballer, Duncan Shepherd, Albert, Les Welch, Tony Minshall, John Ball Celebrity Charity match.

*Farouk Engineer (Wicket keeper and batsman) Cyril Forrester,
Les Welch and Albert.*

*Sparks; L-R: Cyril Forrester,Robert Williams, Albert,
Paul Squires, Tony Hateley.*

Paul Henry.

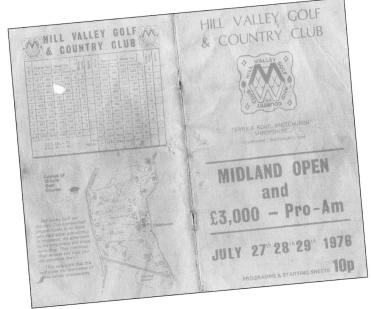

John Stokes, Willie Morgan, Johnny Mathis and Albert at Hill Valley.

13th Tee:
The Staff Of Hill Valley Golf Club And Hotel

13th Hole - Par 5 - 477 yards

The easiest of the par 5 holes on the course but still holds its own; the tee shot requires the ball to be hit down the right hand side of the fairway at what the members call the goal posts (two oak trees) as the fairway slopes from left to right towards the line of conifer trees. The green may be within range in two but a stream 20 yards short collects those that don't make it, pot bunkers either side of the green collect way ward shots.

"A business can't be built up unless you've got the right staff around you."

Albert.

"You can't do enough for a good boss and I think that applies 100% to Albert. People work for him. He's always pleasant. Like his golf, he's always competitive but never aggressive."

Tony Hateley

"One of Albert's great strengths is good delegation."

Bob Walker

CYRIL EDGE

Early one morning in 1972, Albert went for a walk across his newly acquired farmland, visualising the great championship course that would one day spread across the rolling acres. Away in the distance he observed a solitary figure apparently digging away in a hedgerow ditch. He wandered over and found there an elderly chap who, with a Woodbine cigarette clenched firmly between his teeth, was working hard clearing out the ditch.

"What are you up to?" enquired Albert.

The elderly man didn't even bother to look up. He just mumbled that he was clearing out the ditch.

"What's your name then?" asked Albert

"Cyril." Was the reply.

"Who do you work for?" continued Albert.

"I dunna really know, but I'm told some young fella has

Cyril Edge.

Psalm 37 Verse 25

I was young and now I am old, yet I haven't never seen the righteous forsaken or their children begging bread

bought this place and is going to build a golf course here."

Albert continued, "Who's been paying you then?"

"No-one. I ain't bin paid for a month or so" replied the old man.

Albert then told him that he was the young man who had bought the land and he was indeed going to build a golf course. He had taken a liking to the old man and said he would be very happy if Cyril could carry on with his work. Cyril lived with his two sisters in one of the Terrick cottages on Albert's new land. They had not known what the sale of the land and cottages would mean for their futures. Together Albert and Cyril quickly settled on a deal. Albert told him straight away that they could all stay there rent free for their lifetime and then they agreed a weekly payment of £13 and a couple of hundred Woodbines a week. Cyril was very happy and thanked Albert.

"I don't need much. I got the pension so I don't need much at all."

This arrangement continued for many years and Cyril became a familiar face around Hill Valley Golf Club. He could be seen walking out early every morning with his rake on his back. He never used a buggy for transport or any motorised machine for his work. His tools were a scythe and a rake and his beautifully raked bunkers were renowned. He died of pneumonia in the late 1980's. His cottage had become known as 'Woodbine Cottage'.

"For all those years I knew Cyril, I learnt so much from him. I don't suppose that Cyril ever left Whitchurch but he was one special character and it's been the special characters that have come and gone and stayed at Hill Valley that make the place so special."

Old Cyrils' House renovated for Albert. 1989.

PETER CONDLIFFE:

"Peter helped a lot in building up the business."
Albert

"I was 27 years old when I met Albert in 1972. I had arrived in Shropshire as an out of work trained caterer. My girlfriend, the daughter of a local beautician, said she knew of a local businessman in Wem who was planning a golf course and why didn't I go and see him. So I rang him up and asked for an appointment. I didn't realise at the time that he owned half of Wem. I went to meet him at his office and I can see him clearly now. He was wearing brown shoes with the heels that were fashionable at that time and cavalry twill flared trousers and a checked sports jacket and he sat on the radiator at the windowsill in his office for the whole interview.

"I'm an out of work caterer," I said, "have you got a job for me?"

"Well the golf course won't be ready for three years," he replied, "but I'm just about to buy a building in the centre of Wem and I'd like to turn it into a steak bar. If you can set it up and run it for me for the next three years then you've got a job at the end of that at the golf club."

I told him I lived a little far away and he said that's no problem, I've got a big house you can come and live with my family for six months. And this was all in half an hour. I'd never met him before, he didn't ask where I had been before and he didn't ask for any references. He just took me on at face value. You see I was not just an out of work caterer, I was a coloured out of work caterer, a son of immigrants and that was forty years ago when attitudes to people like me were very difficult and there was a lot of prejudice around. He looked through the colour of my skin. He looked me in the eye and listened to me and he said, "Well I like what I see in you, you're my sort of man," and that's it. The deal was done. In the first half hour of meeting him he set up a company with me being a 25% shareholder and no costs, no references. He had five children and I shared a bedroom with his eldest lad and I was just like one of his family straight away from off the street. It gave me so much confidence. He creates loyalty and gives opportunities and everything he said he would do for me he did. If you can look him in the eye, he listens to what you say. Then he makes a judgement on you not on what your reputation is.

Peter Condliffe, Beryl, Albert and Brenda Condliffe.

Bill and Olive Furber, lifelong friends of Albert and Beryl.

He sees when people can contribute and then makes them successful at that. He is a risk taker with vision to make money for other people. He developed a team in those early days at Hill Valley and so much of the team are still there. He looks in your heart and if he feels your heart is in the right place then he can work with you and if your heart is in the right place that's all he asks for and to trust him. If you do that, you can conquer anything. Very few people have that ability to make people believe in themselves and feel great.

I used to join Albert when he went out in the evenings to the local pubs. I noticed very quickly that there were no pretensions with him. He'd talk to anyone from landowners to dustbin men. If I was with him, I'd just be left there, he wouldn't give a fig if I knew anyone or not and what I realised is that he is like a free spirit, you can't contain him, he's happy like that. He'd find out so much about peoples lives, intimate things too, because he was a good listener. He made people feel that what they said was important. I never felt inferior because like the others, Albert was always interested in what you had to say and he always felt he could learn from anyone.

When Hill Valley opened in 1975 I was the catering manager and I also ran the nightclub in the old stables that had been converted. We used to put on many, many events. For example, it might be a Norwegian evening with Norwegian food and I would paint the walls and decorate the whole place. Because we were a new company and a new club we attracted a lot of local people and many people met there and then later they got married. I became catering director after 15 years. I shared a flat with Tony in the Hill Valley grounds and lived there for ten years.

At 7 or 8 o'clock in the morning Albert would be right there outside my window wanting to know how the evening before had gone or with some new idea and I'd only got to bed at 3am. But I would be up and ready. I worked 7 days a week and never had a day off in 5 years, but I just wanted to be part of it all and listen to what he said. I would weed the greens even though I was catering manager. I would do cartwheels for him and enjoy it, he enthused me.

Albert, with his brilliant brain, would have the ideas and inspirations, make calculations on the back of a fag packet, although he never smoked, and then Les would work those ideas through. I have fantastic respect for him as a businessman. He had intuition. Seeing those fields in 1972 and having the vision and the vitality to carry it through. He always had the support of his wonderful wife, Beryl, but no one had any influence on him. We had to follow him; he demands support but he gives it back. He likes things to be just right. He changed the pro shop and cloakrooms many times to get them right. He had foresight and visionary ideas for the new clubhouse, some of which the council planning squashed, which was a shame. It would have been ahead of its time. So he's had his share of set backs but he carries himself and everyone forward with him.

He's never been a scholar. He's made mistakes but he's had a fascinating journey. That's it with Albert. It's not what you get, it's how you get there. It's the journey that has been his degree with him.

I went to catering college and Albert would sometimes make some sandwiches and he'd proudly bring them to me to show me. They were very good, his sandwiches were great but he wasn't interested in it. He respected my love and my skills for my work.

I left three times but I couldn't escape and I went back three times. Once I went back to him for half the money just for the excitement of working for him. I was just as happy being an employee at Hill Valley for Albert as I am now running my own business. Thirty years on we're still like the best of mates. Albert took me to church just last week. I'm very fortunate to have met him.

I hated golf. I would play and get so frustrated and see others frustrated. But living at Hill Valley, I would see Albert practising his swing and I learnt what you had to do, so even though I couldn't play I began to teach some of the juniors. It's a stupid game! But I went all over Europe and I caddied for Tony and I loved every minute of it. I could recognise the talent Tony had and he had so much golfing ability but he didn't have the heart. Ian had talent and the heart and that made him a winner. Both are great golfers but one was a winner.

Jack Nicklaus was quoted as saying, "The harder you work the luckier you get". You make your own luck and Albert has done that.

He's a unique character, but a lovable one. He's got so much time for everybody. I can't speak highly enough of him. He's an inspiration to others.

He took a coloured immigrant lad in to live with him and his five children and wife, forty years ago and that was wonderful. I would die for him."

Peter now owns and runs 'The Station Grill' at Llanysantffraid in Wales, where he still brings international menus and evenings to his own restaurant with the imagination and flair that he brought to the restaurant at Hill Valley for so many years. When Ian Woosnam won the Masters in the USA in

1992, he rang Peter and asked him to cater for a large celebration dinner. Peter was able to put his imaginative talents to great use for his former bottle-up boy and created an evening of splendour and design. The Buffet table was 13th fairway at Augusta with its Tee and dogleg, its pine and cypress trees including the cascading waterfall at the corner green displaying all the sweets. A lady carved out of ice with a red cape around her under a pagoda of flowers dispensed champagne. There was a bust made out of chocolate of Ian winning the Masters and commemoration mugs from the potteries in Stoke.

GRAEME BAGNALL

In 1986, when he was 16, Graeme applied to be a golfer under the government's new Youth Training Scheme. He was sent to meet Albert at Hill Valley and a game of golf was arranged with Andrew. Albert offered him a job immediately and Graeme, the first YTS golf trainee in the country, began as a shop assistant in the pro shop while Albert and Hill Valley developed his golfing skills and gave him the chance to play. In 1992 Graeme turned professional playing off a handicap of 1. He travelled all over the world playing golf sponsored by Albert. He sponsored both Andrew and Graeme, the entry for their first professional tournament as well as £2500 expenses. When Graeme won his first cheque for £400 he immediately offered it straight back to Albert. Albert refused it saying,' No thank you. It's your first cheque. You've won it, now you keep it. It's yours'.

Graeme remembers one Pro Am tour in Portugal when he and his team mates were a little worse for wear after a long evening out. Albert, who was known for never buying or drinking alcohol himself, got up early, went to the local supermarket and bought a six pack of beer for each lad, placing it on their buggies as 'hair of the dog' to make them feel better during the morning play.

"You lads need this," Albert said knowing they had been out all night.

"We played marvellously that morning!" laughs Graeme.

"He's been like a second dad. He took me on when he met me, aged 16, and treated me as part of the family straight away. He included me on family holidays. Andrew and I became good friends and were best man to each other. Albert's got so many qualities. He's friendly, generous and he never gets cross. I've done a bit of everything at Hill Valley from demolition to working on the greens in the winter months to just whatever is needed to help around the whole place and be a part of Hill Valley. I've never even thought of moving away. You could say that it's the staff that have helped make Albert but the truth is Albert has given so much to his staff, in so many ways. That has really been the story of Hill Valley. Some corporations can't keep their staff for twenty to thirty days. Well, we've all been here twenty to thirty years."*

In 1997 Graeme made the decision to return to amateur status and concentrate on developing his role as manager of the pro shop at Hill Valley.

*Sandra France worked for 25 years in the restaurant, David Parks for many years as the chef and Angelina Edge has worked for eighteen years as a cleaner in the hotel.

JAMIE MINSHALL

Jamie, Tony's son is the third generation of Minshall to join Hill Valley as a staff member. He was encouraged to play golf as a youngster and played in several tournaments but decided not to pursue life as a professional golfer. He joined Hill Valley as a green keeper in 1998, moving into the pro shop in 2000 and in 2004 became a director of golf for MacDonalds UK. In 2005 Jamie became golf manager at Hill Valley.

His grandfather and father have been great influences in his life instilling in him the importance of being up and getting things done very early in the morning on a golf course. He has grown up with and been part of the personal and hands on manner in which Albert and Tony have run Hill Valley, the dedication and loyalty of so many of the staff, the care and personal consideration given to members and guests. He sees the value of and wants to continue, the family connection, from Albert saying good morning to the guests at breakfast to sitting and having a chat to a group of golfers in the evening.

THE GREEN KEEPERS OF HILL VALLEY GOLF COURSE

"The greens were magnificent, they were the best greens I'd ever played on. The green keepers cut it so well. A 4 wood from 180 yards, hit it in the air and when it landed it would stop dead."

Tony Hateley

Peter Condliffe, Roger Millington, Henry Millington, Mike Evans, Maurice Reeves overlooking first starting hut. 1970's.

MAURICE REEVES

"Albert and I have known each other since Sunday School. We did such a lot together. We both played football at Whixall; he was a better footballer than me and got into the team as goalkeeper. We played cricket together for Cotonhall in the grounds of the Cotonhall estate and farmland belonging to Lord Hill. We would bike to the railway station in Wem and go to watch matches at Shrewsbury. After the matches we would go into town for fish and chips and into 'The Quarry' to watch a wrestling match. Then we would catch the train back to Wem, get our bikes and finish up dancing at the local hall. That was our Saturdays. That was our summers for many years. Then as we grew up and got married we stayed friends but went our different ways. I went into farming and Albert went into the building business. And every time I met him he would say, 'why don't you come to me?'

'I don't know anything about the building business', I would reply.

'Well you can learn' he said.

Well, I stayed in farming. Then one day, 1n 1974, I was at the garage Albert owned in Wem, filling the car with petrol and he came over and said, 'You're the fellow I want.'

'What for?'

'On that golf course.'

'Well, I've never set foot on a golf course. I don't know a thing about golf, being in farming.'

'Oh, you'll soon learn. Will you come and cut the fairways for me?'

'All right.' I replied and I went. It was all strange to me after working with cattle. They had only just got the greens and fairways laid, with grass just coming up. Ron Smith was the green keeper and I worked under him for twelve months. The day before he left Albert came up to me and said, 'You're green keeper from tomorrow'

Greenkeeper's workings.

111

I said 'Good Lord! I don't know anything',
'Well you'll have to learn, won't you.' he replied.

So I got all these green keeper books and I read it all up, irrigation and everything and I was head green keeper. They opened the course in June 1975, I got married that September and Albert was my best man at my wedding.

Those early days were very hard work and there were some struggles but Albert would always come and talk to me. Every morning he would be sitting waiting for us at the workman's shed and we would talk about everything, what needed doing and how best to do it. I felt we were building something together and that I was part of it all. That's how it went on through the years. He made me a director around 1976 and I was head green keeper for twenty-five years. I never missed farming; I never looked back.

When I arrived, the land looked quite like a desert, with just about just about 20 oak trees scattered about. We spent all that first winter and the year after planting trees, thousands of trees. We laid the fairways and Albert used to say, 'I'll just leave it to you, not too regimental, put a bit of shape in'.

The machinery has altered so much now. There was no cab on the tractor, so we got wet through all day. I spent all day walking up and down with a fertilizer pack on my back and a little rotary spray. Now they have a large automatic spreader spray machine and the job is done much more quickly.

We did any job that needed doing. In the winter we helped with all the building work including the conversion building of Terrick Hall Hotel.

The clubhouse moved six times when I was there. We'll have it up here they'd say. Then it would come down again. It never stopped!

Albert was always looking out for new and better things

At one time on the course we had made pot style bunkers. Albert went to Spain on a golf tour and he came back and said, 'I've seen something different. Let's try it this new way.' So we changed all the bunkers from pot bunkers to a larger more shallow style. We would always be changing and improving the course.

During the 1980's we extended the 9-hole course into an 18, levelling the ground and planting. Then Albert sold the land and it went back to a 9-hole. We took all the bunkers out, put the fences back up and the new owner planted it for cattle. Then about seven years later Albert re-bought the land and we had to dig it all over again and re-make the 18-hole course. The fences came down, the ground had to be dug and levelled and sown all over again. I sowed the greens by hand with a sowing fiddle. From a field to a golf course twice over.

One year, a swan built a nest on the island in the middle of the lake on the 8th fairway. It was exactly where players' golf balls would often land so Albert asked us to build a shield to protect the swan. It worked well and the swan and her mate had many, many young ones. Each year the players would ask, 'any babies yet?' The swan family would walk right across the course. The male swan would lead with the signets in the middle and the female at the back. The golf players used to bring their camcorders and film them waddling up the fairways. Albert started feeding them on the 18th green but he had to stop because they got so cheeky they would march right up to the clubhouse and peck at the club door while the players were having their breakfast.

I would be working on the green, moving the flags or something and the male and female swans would walk the signets up to the top of a mound beside the green or the bunker and flap their wings. The signets would watch and copy them. Many times I watched them pecking their young to leave and sending them away from the nest.

Canada geese used to come and torment the swans so I would go up there in the evenings at around 8pm in my land rover to check the swans were all right and try and get the geese to fly away.

One freezing winter the signets had flown the nest and there was only the male and female there. They were stranded in the house in the middle of the pond because of all the snow and ice. The Fire Brigade came out to get the swans off the pond and we gave them some food. The swans took to sleeping in the bunker finding the sand under the snow. I arrived early one morning to see all these feathers about. A fox had bitten off the male's head. The female survived. She did meet another mate and had just had one more brood but no more after that. A fox walked across the ice and killed all the ducks on their island as well. I grieved for the swan.

But oh, the rabbits! In the morning we'd be going to mow the greens and we'd have to weave around hundreds of them and they would just sit and watch us. Albert loves all of them being there. It's part of the golf course for him.

There was a pile of sand on the land that Albert had tested. It was good sand and he sold it well but when the buyer came to take it all away they found Sand Martin's, nesting inside it. So Albert sent the buyer away until the next winter came and the birds had safely flown away.

Whenever I dug all the borders around the clubhouse there would be Robins and blackbirds sitting on my spade, catching the worms as I dug them up.

Head Green keeper was a lovely job and a hard job. The players were always friendly and polite as I used to dodge around them mowing the greens. I was struck twice in 25 years by golf balls. I was moving the flags on the green and one hit my head and knocked me right out. The second one was on a foggy day and it hit my chest. I dropped to my knees on the green thinking that I'd had a heart attack.

Albert tried to get me to play golf but I wouldn't. I said, 'no I'm not starting because if I do I'll never see my wife'.

Albert would always come to me if he had any problem. We would sit down on the grass and he'd say, 'What do you think Maurice?' He'd always listen to me and be interested in what I thought. 'I don't really know what to do, what's your opinion?' he would ask. Not just about the golf course but business as well. He valued my opinion and that was nice.

We never had any disputes and there was no problem ever going from being a friend to working for him. He'd come to me on the course and we'd sit in the sun and have a talk. He would put his arm around me and say, 'Let's get it done'.

Everything he touched seemed to turn to gold. I used to say to him, 'One of these days you're going to hit oil,' and it wouldn't have surprised me if he had!

About six months ago, Albert came up to me and said, 'I could just do with you now, you know, we're busy'. At this, Maurice laughed heartily

"I can't start now, I'm full of arthritis!" he chuckled.

"In twenty-five years, apart from the day the swans died, I never ever came home unhappy.

We were all one happy family. It worked good."

ALBERT ABOUT THE PRESENT GREEN KEEPERS

"Mike Evans is our head green keeper now and I would say he's the best green keeper in the country. Roger Millington, David Minshall and Peter Ankers work with him and these are the vital men on the course now. Four of the best men as you could ever get on a golf course. I rely on them to do all the jobs and work on any alterations and improvements. A lot of credit has got to be given to all these people over the years. We say we built it but those lads have worked hard and many have been here since they were 16 and are still here today."

MIKE EVANS joined Hill Valley on June 21st 1975 just before its completion. He was 16 years old and training to be a rig diver. After rupturing an eardrum during a diving training session he then remained at Hill Valley full-time becoming Head Green Keeper in 1995. ROGER MILLINGTON joined 9 months after Mike in 1976, DAVID MINSHALL also joined in 1976 and PETER ANKERS began working at Hill Valley in the early 1980's.

Peter Ankers, Roger Millington, Dave Minshall, Mike Evans (Head Greenkeeper). Greenkeepers 2006.

MIKE EVANS, ROGER MILLINGTON AND DAVID MINSHALL

"More often than not, he isn't happy unless we're digging holes for him or moving soil. That's when Albert is at his happiest. He likes any type of construction work being done. He just likes digging, he can't stand still, he likes making new things, and something has got to be altered. We don't know why he has a golf course because he just likes digging!

When the land that has become the Sapphire course was bought in 1976 the grass was very high and there were 500 sheep grazing. Albert took us up onto the land. He had the plan for the course in his head.'Right,' he said, 'we'll start by digging here and digging there. We'll have a bunker here and a tee over there. Go and get me half a dozen pegs and we'll knock 'em in'. Later he would drive up in his Rolls Royce and if he liked the results of the digging he would drive happily on by.

There are six full time staff for 2 18-hole courses. Nearby golf courses have got around 37 staff for 2 18-hole courses but they nearly all get laid off in the winter. But we are here all winter; we don't get cut off work ever. There's always something to look after, something always needs changing or mending. In the summer the cutting never stops and there's lots of irrigation work to do. We always think it's going to go quiet but it never does, something always strikes up. Now the only thing is don't mention holidays! 'Oh no! What do you want a holiday for?' he'll say, 'can't you have it when it's raining?'

He's always been one for being out early in the morning. When we first worked here he'd always be out at half past six in the morning. He would drive around the whole course and the golfers would see this white Rolls Royce appearing by the greens and fairways. We were always there working early and he always liked to come and see us and have a chat but I never felt he was checking up on us. He likes getting any new business done by ten o'clock. Then at the end of every day he'd always come and check with us that our day had gone all right and we were happy with everything.

We've always been treated all right. We've had a good job with him. He's looked after us. We've grown up with him. We understand him and are that used to him and we know his ways, we know how he ticks. We know to keep away from him and let him be if his head is down into his shoulders.

He's very generous. I don't mean money. When I was building my new house I came to him and asked if I could borrow the tractor and the digger. 'You have those as much as you like,' he said, 'they're as much yours as they are mine.' And he would never take a penny off any of us for anything like that.

He lends us his car, his Rolls and everything, as much as we want. We've been to many golf shows in his Rolls.

One Sunday morning I was driving the Rolls back home to him and a car crashed into me and there was quite a bit of damage to the front. I rang him to tell him. I didn't mind ringing him, he was having his dinner at the time. 'Are you all right?' He asked. 'As long as you are all right that's the main thing. I can always replace the car,' and he came out and looked and saw it was quite a mess so he took it away. A few weeks later he had a new car and he drove in and threw me the keys. 'Go on,' he said, 'go and take the car or else you won't drive it again will you!'

We've all travelled a bit with him to Spain and Montenegro but he can't get us off the course here. We've been here that long we know what we're doing, we don't need any plans and we don't want to be working over there now.

We planted every tree on this golf course with our own hands. In 1976 Albert took a gang of us up to Knutsford where we dug up 80.000 small trees from a nursery, brought them all to Hill Valley and planted them close together because we thought we'd lose a quarter of them but they all grew.

It's changed a bit here now, there are contracts and things like that, that there didn't used to be. We've always done any work necessary all around Hill Valley like building, knocking down walls and putting in lintels. We've done a bit of everything, helped out wherever it's needed. He tends to get retrospective planning always because all the red tape slows everything down so it drives him mad with frustration. 'Why make everything so awkward?' he asks. He has so many ideas so sometimes he tells us to forget what we're doing at that moment and go and start this new idea. 'Let's do it now,' he'll say! He'd sooner have his own men because we can read his mind and he won't have any mither. And he'd have to have plans as well with new men. With us he can just say do that over there and we know what he wants. He'll say, 'we'll have a pond here, go and dig it out,' and I ask him what sort of shape and he says, 'oh well, you know.' Or a bunker, he'll, say, just tell me to make it kidney shaped or heart shaped. His mind works overtime about the golf course. You know he'll say, 'I woke up at three or four-o'clock in the morning and I was thinking about that bunker!' It's his life. He's done so much for this place.

He's got a very kind way with him, if any one starts ranting and raving or raising their voice he'll just walk away from them. Or he'll say, 'calm down my friend, there's no need to speak loudly.' If there's a problem he'll say, 'well there's a way round it. There's always a way round everything. We don't want obstacles.'

He's never sworn at us. Of course over the years we've had disagreements about things but never cross words and we have never fallen out. He can change his mind a lot and we know how to work with him on that because we're used to it. We just take no notice!

He'd help anybody. In the early days there used to be an old shed, on what was the practice ground, beside the old railway line. We used to brew up our tea in there and light a fire in the winter to keep us warm. One morning a tramp came slithering down the hay and straight out of the upper floor opening and landed on the ground beneath. Albert happened to be passing by and saw this and went up to him as the old fellow was on his way and gave him £20.

When my father was poorly and I said I had to go and see my dad, he said to me, 'you just park the tractor up and go' and he wouldn't mind one bit, 'take all the time you need', he'd say and he has never knocked any hours off us for anything and he never has done. Any overtime we always get paid, whatever hours we do, no qualms. He does like a deal though and I've seen him flip a coin to settle a price.

The golfers always love to see him. No matter what society is here he'll always go straight up to them and start talking to them. He'll sit on the wall in the car park or lean against his car and go over and have a conversation with them. He probably talks a load of rubbish to them but they love it and when they come back the following year they always ask if the old boss is here. He makes them feel special. Of course if somebody will talk about golf to him he'll talk to them all day! He always has the ladies laughing. He has the gift of the gab and they like him. He gets them to hit their ball over his car to practice a shot!

People come and shake our hands and have a chat. But our own members moan the worst. If they moan too much Albert says, 'Well shall we give you your money back?' They all come up and tell us what we ought to be doing; they all think they know better. We say nothing. We just agree because they're the customers and they are paying our wages. The other thing is they'll always come and tell you when it's bad but they'll never come and say anything when it's good. They'll moan about their wet shoes but we don't round 'em up, force them to go out in it!

But the members all know us over the years and they all come over and speak to us or give us a wave and always have done so. And you see, with a lot of the visiting golfers, they see Albert coming over and talking to us and how he is with us and it helps because Albert will always talk to us lads and the golfers then see us in a different light. I've seen many who won't talk to us at all and then they see Albert talking to us and only then will they come over and talk to us. I suppose they think well if we're good enough for Albert to talk to then they'll come and speak to us. We see that with a lot of golfers.

He won't have anything killed. Rabbits cause us havoc digging great big holes in the bunkers. We've got 400-500 rabbits living very happily at Hill Valley. They won't even move away they're that used to people. Rabbits dig their escape route just under the turf so golfers suddenly disappear. There have been broken ankles and all sorts of trouble. We've had whole machines disappear. The rabbits don't go on the greens. Except the 15th, one summer one particular rabbit liked the 15th.

Albert feeds the baby ducks from the red buggy so they all run after the red buggy when they see it moving.

He's a very talented golfer, he walks straight up to a tee and he hits the ball straight down the middle. He picked it up from nothing. Even at his age now he can hit it long as some of the youngsters. He's very gifted how things seem to come to him.

He never misses chapel and even told the taxman once that, 'none of this is mine,' and 'my friend is helping me with this'. That really foxed the man until Albert explained that he meant God.

When he took a bang on his head he said, 'get my lads off the course and get the car and I want them to take me to hospital'. He didn't want any ambulance; he just wanted us, his lads.

We've had some laughs over the years. One morning Albert hadn't seen a lawn mower on the green and he drove straight into it and pushed it off the green with his car. Another time his Rolls got stuck on practice field and we had to get the JCB to pull it off for him."

John and Albert.

JOHN MINSHALL

John, Albert's older brother also joined the team part time during the planting and developing of the land at Hill Valley in the 1976. He remembers helping lay the paths with a young Ian Woosnam, who he remembers as a gifted lad.

John recognizes that he and Albert are 'as chalk and cheese'.

"Albert is a risk taker who could never stand still. I worried too much. He was gifted at sport as a young man and then in business too but he never rested much. He's worked hard. He hasn't changed though, from those early days right until now. He has always known so many of the local people and they supported him in the early days and still do. He'll still talk to everybody as an equal and make sure they are doing all right and if they aren't he'll go and do something about it!"

BOB WALKER

A founder member and from 1980-1998 he worked as the 'Golf Administrator' at Hill Valley.

"It was utopia working at Hill Valley. We had such good banter, Albert and I and he's such a kind man. I loved cricket and played for Whitchurch in my youth. One day Albert asked me to play golf in a tournament and he had arranged for Johnny Wardle, one of my cricketing heroes to be my partner. I had such a good time.'

BERNARD SIERTSEMA

A founder member at Hill Valley Golf Club.

"I don't know what it is about Hill Valley but I just love this place. I love being here and I love working here. I've done a bit of everything, working wherever I was needed."

At present Bernard works as a concierge in the new hotel reception

CHAUFFEUR: JIMMY GRAY

"I've always wanted their philosophy to rub off on me.

You couldn't hope to meet better people as employers. They're like friends. Everything Albert has done has been through hard work; nothing was handed to him on a plate.

I've seen it all grow from an acorn to a large tree and it's all down to Albert. He had foresight and took risks. He's a character and that's been part of its success.

He's a millionaire but he doesn't act like it and he will help anyone.

I remember one time when I had been caddying for them at the Spanish Open and we were coming back on the plane. Albert got chatting, as he always liked to do, to an elderly couple who had just finished their first and only holiday abroad. They had saved for years just for that one holiday and although they loved it, they couldn't afford another one. Albert sent them a cheque covering the cost of another holiday. He gave them a holiday. He'd never met them before.

It's in their genes. Material things aren't the most important things for Albert."

Jonathan Lomas - Tour Professional attached to Hill Valley.

Hill Valley Golf & Country Club

TERRICK ROAD, WHITCHURCH, SHROPSHIRE
Telephone Whitchurch (01948) 663584 & 667788 Fax (01948) 665927

27th May 1998

Robert

Dear Robert

Official Retirement

Well Robert the time has come to throw out our crow quill and let the youth and the computers take over.

We can stand or sit back and reflect would we have done any thing different with modern technology or would the new breed have had the success we've had, interesting times.

Seriously though Bob, I would like to take this opportunity to officially thank you for all your work and interest in helping to establish Hill Valley to its current position.

No doubt your involvement with us won't finish with your retirement at the end of May and we still look forward to maintaining our friendship links in the future.

In recognition of your special endeavours I would like you to accept this voucher to put towards a Green or Summerhouse from myself and fellow Directors.

Best wishes

Albert

Albert Minshall

Owners: A.J. Minshall Ltd.
Directors: A.J. Minshall (Chairman), A.R. Minshall (Vice Chairman), L. Welch (Managing Director), B. Minshall (Secretary), C.L. Forrester.
Shareholders: A.J. Minshall, Jnr., M.L. Welch

Bob Walker retirement letter.

14th Tee:

Running A Golf Club

14th Hole - Par 4 - 357 yards

If down the wind the pro's can drive the green here but sensibly lay up short of the tree on the left and miss the ditch on the right leaving a short iron in to the green, this looks quite flat but local knowledge says there is a severe slope from right to left.

"I suppose like most other people I am basically idle and if you have to work it might as well be at something you enjoy."

Albert

"I've never ever seen Albert lose his temper. He's had reason to many times. He's got a bit sort of ruffled occasionally but he's laid back you see, he saunters away."

**Bob Walker, Membership Secretary
1977-1992**

"Well, for a start, out of 400 members, I've got 200 green keepers."

Albert

"Many people say to me what a wonderful thing it must be to own a golf course. What an easy job! You just go around and collect the green fee money off the players and people come and stay in your hotel. Well of course, that's the biggest load of nonsense isn't it! It's a very hard job. People come up to me and say well I should be doing this or that or the greens should be this way or that way or I should be putting this or that on them. Out of 400 members I've got 200 telling me how to run the place. So I've just continued doing it my way and that's how I've always done it.

Everyone thinks we've made millions. I've lost millions running a golf club! I wouldn't consider the golf course a success from a financial point of view. I had a wonderful building and property development business and that's where I really made my money. The difference between making a lot of money, which I did in the early years and then running a golf course, is enjoying life. It's been a very happy time. That's the thing I

Albert.

go back and look at. I've enjoyed creating a golf club. I chose to do something I like doing. I liked building but I chose something where I could meet more people and have a bit more fun and I haven't regretted that. Perhaps I should have carried on and built more golf courses in the early years and not stopped at running just one. We've talked many times in meetings as to whether we should continue and buy more land and build more courses. We were good at building our first course and probably reasonably good, perhaps not the best in the world, at running it. But then I look back at all the people who have worked for me and these are the lads who have made the course. They feel a sense of ownership with it and that's good, although I know that none of us own anything, we're just here for a while to look after something. We are all general managers but the feeling of ownership makes us care for the land we're working on. The green keepers work very hard, arriving at 5 in the morning and cutting the greens. They're always here. Not many people will do that. I trust them to do the job. So therefore we have a good relationship. I consider them as friends; they work with me not for me. That's how we've always done it. Look at wonderful old Cyril. He worked all hours for a few quid. He loved to meet you in the mornings with his rake on his back. He always walked everywhere; he never drove anywhere. Today they all fly around in buggies. You must have people working for you who have a real interest and if they haven't then they're better off doing something else. You can't run a business unless you've got good people with you and that's what I've always tried to do.

With a golf course, people come to play and they appreciate a well-run club. They become good friends and then spread good word about the golf club and slowly the business and reputation builds in many areas. And it's all done on goodwill and friendship. For a successful business with a golf club you must have good friends all around you and if you do a good job you'll always get custom. You've got to enjoy talking to many different people. This morning, I've been around the dining room talking to all the golfers and having a chat about different methods to improve a game, and this is it; I go and see them in the dining room or at breakfast time and say hello to them and I make quite sure that all is well and if anything is wrong, if there are any problems, then I go and tell whoever is the person to put it right. That's my method of working. How good you are is shown by the customers you have. That's how we work.

As for building a golf course, well I'm sitting here looking out onto the 9th tee and I can see how all the trees have grown

Skiing at Hill Valley in the snow.

over the years. We can't do that. That's all been done by nature. In the 1970's, Alex Lyle told me it would take twenty years for the course to achieve maturity. He was right. Actually, it's taken a bit longer to get it into a mature golf course. Ours has been open 31 years and I think now it's pretty good.

I would say I would change the way we went about it. We didn't know enough about it all. If I started to build a golf course now I would like to begin with more vision about how I would like it to have developed after ten years. I didn't know enough about that when we built Hill Valley. I would advise anyone planning to build a golf course now to get very good advice. But they have to sift the real advice from people who don't really know but think that they do. Tony and Andrew are finding the same things building their new golf courses in Montenegro. The new fast growing grass seed that takes only 3 to 4 years to reach maturity on golf courses doesn't answer all the questions.

There's one other thing I've learnt running a golf course and that's always to be very careful what you say out loud anywhere, especially in the bar or dining area. You never know who is listening. I'm careful not to talk too loud and I'll warn people who are talking too loud when they have had a few drinks. I've learnt to listen before I speak when I first meet someone so that I know whom it is that I am dealing with. Instead of talking too much, keep quiet for a bit. You can always have your say later.

Would I change much running a golf business? Well, you make what you think is the best decision you can possibly make at the time but there will always be regrets; everybody has regrets. I regret not spending more time with my five children. I was working hard and trying to make money and I was ambitious, too ambitious probably. If I got my time to go over again, I would definitely change that side. I would spend more time with my children when they were young. I've got a wonderful wife who did spend the time at home with them.

Running a golf business? It's not all sunshine."

PART THREE

15th Tee:

Beryl and the Family.

15th Hole - Par 3 - 178 yards

Standing on the elevated tee the tee shot is quite tight to what looks a simple large target, miss the green either side and one of the five deep bunkers will collect the ball.

"Knowing that someone is waiting up for you with a sandwich and a cup of tea. Now that's worth a fortune."

Albert

"Always have enough money for your wife to have her hair permed. Then you can go and enjoy a game of golf."

Albert

"You must have a woman there beside you if you are going to be successful. Who, whatever happens, will stay the course beside you for fifty years."

Albert

BERYL ABOUT ALBERT

When Albert first came and knocked on the door of Beryl's home in Prees her father answered.

"There's a chap wants to see you." Beryl's father said.

"Tell him to go away. I don't want to see him," Replied Beryl out of shyness more than anything else, although Albert did have some reputation as a rather wild young lad who liked his drink.

"No, I can't tell him to go away," said her father.

So Beryl reluctantly went to meet the chap at the door. They sat and chatted for a while and were married six months later in 1956. From the beginning to the present day it has been a supportive marriage and partnership.

In the early days Albert's passion was football, fishing and cricket with no golf in sight. Beryl encouraged Albert's golf after his illness in 1964, which was also when he gave up alcohol that he rarely touches today.

Beryl knew from the beginning that Albert was a man who liked to take risks and would 'go for it'. She believes strongly that marriage is about supporting her husband and never minded that golf and business kept him away and so busy. "He always came home," she smiles. She trusted in and supported his vision. She looks back on the Hawkstone years as happy times but she knew that for Albert,

"It was his dream to have his own golf course."

Louise, Wendy, Carol, Rosie Welch, Andrew, Albert and Beryl.

BERYL

"I've done a lot of things, met some interesting people and travelled. I wouldn't say there have been hard times, no. Somehow things always seemed to slot into place so we were never desperate. I think that's because Albert is such an honest man. He believes things will come right and they generally do. He never treats anybody in a way he would not wish to be

130

treated himself. People he works with are very loyal to him because he's the sort of man who engenders loyalty.

We're coming towards the end of his dream. We're getting things finished off. Everything Albert hoped for or expected is being fulfilled. It's a lovely ending and another beginning. Everything is going to be lovely, we hope. It's been fun being part of it, part of his dream."

Reflecting on her life, their family and Albert's great achievements, Beryl is extremely modest about her role in it all, only once conceding with a smile that, "yes at times I was the one to hold them all together".

Beryl played good golf herself but never felt competitive about the game and was very busy with five children. Their children were brought up with the world of golf around them and Tony and Andrew are now building and developing exciting new golf courses and projects in Montenegro.

Beryl and Albert with some of their grandchildren.

BILL SMITH, FAMILY FRIEND, ABOUT BERYL

You'd never meet a more genuine and kind lady than Beryl who has looked after Albert and her family for all these years."

'I think perhaps you shouldn't be a father until you are 70

131

years old. When you get to 70 that's where you learn some common sense and how to be with the children.' Albert

Albert and Beryl have twelve grandchildren* and ten of them have tried golf. Their handicaps range from 1 -36.

Jamie, Tony and Dawn's son plays county scratch 5 handicap and works at Hill Valley. Kelly Lowe, their daughter also works at Hill Valley.

David and Carol Vaughan's son, Jason, is the pro. at Llangollen golf club.

*Tony and Dawn: Jamie, Kelly and Katie
Andrew and Jill: Robyn and William
Carol and David Vaughan: Jason and Jemma
Louise and Kurt Van Flute: Craig, Mark and Faye.
Wendy and David Parkes: Chris and Matthew.

Tony, Andrew and Albert.

Beryl.

Jamie and Craig (Albert's grandsons) with Laura.

Louise.

Jason Vaughan (Grandson).

Cath Forrester, Albert and Beryl.

Wendy, Carol and Louise.

Albert with grandaughters Kelly and Jemma.

Albert with Louise and Kurt at Disney.

Kelly and Tony on Kelly's wedding day.

Kelly's wedding.

Albert and grandaughter Kelly.

16th Tee:

Friends

16th Hole - Par 5 - 490 yards

The key to the hole is the tee shot. A tight fairway is protected by a fairway bunker on the left and a lake stretching up the right hand side find the fairway and the second shot is played to the green over the elevated fairway. A fairway wood or long iron should be the club, the bunker on the right collects wayward shots.

'Everyone has problems but you can talk to a true friend about anything. There are certain pals who remain with you throughout your life.'

Albert

Albert has maintained good friendships with many of his business partners and there are also many life long friends who have not been part of the business, including Wilf and Jean Lyman, Val and Sheila Whiston and a friend who shares Albert's love for fishing, Andy Peate, with whom he fishes twice a week.

Before the building of Hill Valley, in the days when he fished more than he played golf, he shared many happy fishing days with Michael Shuker.

MICHAEL SHUKER

Mick was always known for coming up with ideas and one evening in 1968 Albert called at Mick's house and found him devising a machine to make lead weights for fishing. Albert was interested and asked for a demonstration. The lead had to be melted first and Mick had no saucepan so he quickly used the children's bedtime milk saucepan to melt the lead that evening. Albert invited Mick to set up a small workshop at his yard in New Street, Wem, where he began manufacturing lead weights from there with increasing success.

One day, Albert accompanied Mick to Liverpool, to an interview with the wholesalers, Furshaw's, to try to get an order for his lead weights. Albert noticed Mick had holes in the bottom of his shoes so they quickly lined them with Whitchurch Herald newspaper. During the interview Mick sat crossed legged in front of the managing director, who appeared to spend the

139

entire session reading the paper in the bottom of Mick's shoes. Albert and Mick felt it had not gone well but subsequently Furshaw's offered Mick the biggest order he had ever had.

He became one of the largest lead weight producers in the country. He moved to a new factory, diversified into other fishing tackle and packaging and ran a very successful business. Mick bought himself a house beside a canal where he could 'drop a line whenever he wanted to' and he never lost his early enthusiasm for ideas and inventions. They always laughed together about the hole in the shoes interview.

Some of Albert's happiest golfing memories with friends and family are the Pro Am Tournaments he played in Spain and Portugal with his two sons, Tony and Andrew and Cyril Forrester.

CYRIL FORRESTER

Cyril was born and brought up in Whixall and still lives in Whixall today. From his house he can see across the fields to the house where Albert was born and also the farm that his family moved into a few fields away. He can also see, the first depot from that Albert built for him beside Dobsons Bridge in Whixall. Cyril is another Whixall entrepreneur building up a very successful transport business himself. He and Albert were good friends in both their business and personal lives.

"We played football together for Whixall and Albert was always good at any sport he played. He loved them all. We had a lot of fun on holidays in Blackpool together as young lads. Wherever we were staying, whether it was in a room at the Imperial Hotel or squashed up together in a cheap hostel we always had a lot of fun. Albert could adapt himself happily to any situation. Then when we both married, our wives and families got on very well and we went on many golf trips to Europe together.

It was Albert who encouraged a revival in my playing golf again. I used to play at Llanymynech but I gave it up because it was taking me too much away from my business. I wasn't making any money playing golf so I thought I'd better give it up. Good if you can make money and enjoy playing golf. It's a grand life if you can enjoy what you do!

I go up to Hill Valley now for a cup of tea and a chat with friends, not just to play golf. Golf seems to attract nice people, it's a great leveller because everyone would like to be better and no one is as good as they think they are!

It's good to go through life knowing someone like Albert. It's been a good association both personally and in business. It's all mixed together well. His family has been good to my family especially now to me since losing my wife. You need good friends later on in life. Employees and bosses in corporations all move on and away but businesses in smaller communities don't so much and the Whixall men all still know each other.

I think Hill Valley was a big job to undertake but I think it's all come right. He's conquered it in his way. It's a big asset to the area, bringing in employment and people and it has contributed to Whitchurch in a nice way. I always knew Albert had an eye for business and would see something through. He likes to see people doing well. He was a go ahead person who likes people and likes talking to people. His father was similar like that. Getting on with people is a big thing in life, being able to enjoy a chat.

Albert does a lot of good things for people but he does them in a quiet way, without any mither, without any fuss and without anyone knowing they are done."

BILL SMITH

Bill first met Albert many years ago doing some joinery when he was building houses in Wem. They became close friends during the building of Hill Valley from 1972.

Bill was a builder in opposition but they shared advice and discussed problems and remained friends through the years and have the greatest respect for one another. Bill was made Junior President at Hill Valley in 1975 and looked after the younger players from 1975-1985. "They all used to thrash me at golf." He caddied for Tony at the Spanish Open in La Manga in 1974 and for both Tony and Andrew in many other competitions.

When Hill Valley was opened Albert invited Bill to play golf. Bill was a boxer and he used to hit the balls so hard that no one could ever see where they landed.

"The trouble was, being a boxer, I used to put my right shoulder in. We'd go off searching for my lost balls so many times and Albert would be left standing on a fairway somewhere having to whistle to me so we could try to find each other again. He used to try and give me a few tips and I used to come back in feeling like Quasimodo.

I remember when the Hill Valley course was being built and I'd walk the course with him and I said, 'my word, you should be proud, look at all this,' but he was up out there every morning from 7 in the morning walking the course, looking at the progress, worrying his head and checking every detail.

One thing about Albert is that one minute you're talking with him and the next second you can see he's gone. He'll have suddenly thought of some new idea and you've lost him and he'll say 'I've got to go, I've had an idea' and off he goes. But he's gone to do something about some new idea he's had. In the old days he'd quickly write something down on the back of a fag packet, although he never smoked, so he wouldn't forget. You see, he has great ideas and gets them started, but he likes to hand them over for someone else to see them through. He's a very, very good golfer but he gallops around the course at such a speed. Thinking of the next idea probably.

We've been friends for 50 years, we've been all over the world together, wined and dined and we were always opposition builders and yet we've never had one missed word. I think that's marvellous. Wherever we were in the world, maybe on a golf tour, if you were with Albert you would never have any trouble. He was always very kind. If I've been in trouble he's come to my help. 'William', he says, 'why are you worrying? Your maker will accept you because you're a good man. You've been good to people You've done a lot of good things. You've done a lot of bad things but you've done a lot of good things. He'll take you up there, no question about it.' 'I am worried Rupert*', I reply, I am worried. I don't want to see it's you stoking that fire when I get up there'.

You couldn't wish for a better friend or someone more sincere. Even when he's under a lot of pressure, he has a way with people, he's not aggressive and yet he gets the best out of them all. It's one of his great assets. He never loses his temper. He never likes upsetting anyone or falling out with anybody. Yet he won't be trodden on.

Oh and this chuckle he's got. He'll come out of some serious meeting and he laughs his head off about something or other.

His building business staff stayed with him as much as his Hill Valley staff. I mean, to build up something like he has in his lifetime, from nothing, well, it's a lifetime achievement.

Albert is always cold and he used to wear a big duffle coat. We were out at a pub one night in Bangor and chatting to some ladies who told us they'd visited Hill Valley. I said, 'Well that's the owner over there.' 'Oh yes,' they said looking over at the figure huddled in a duffle coat close to the fire, 'you'll be telling us he owns the Rolls Royce out in the car park next!"

I've seen him many, many times over the years genuinely giving care and time and generosity to his staff or people who are in trouble or ill. Anything he can do for you he will. If he was ever in trouble I tried to go to help him.

We've had such a friendship, even with all this, 'I've had an idea, I've got to get it going,' vanishing in the middle of a conversation. He's a marvel really. Oh we've had some fun."

*Rupert, after Rupert Bear, is Bill's nickname for Albert

STAN CHESTER

Stan Chester grew up in Prees, close to Whixall and knew Albert and his family from an early age. They played football together for Wem Town with Albert in goal and played together in Ruby Owen's team, 'The Sloping Engineers' at Prees. Stan also remembers Albert's good left handed batting in cricket games. Stan became a joiner for Albert's building projects. He was the joiner who built the roof timbers for one of Albert's first houses for his future father in law Alec Harding. Up on the roof Stan would hear Albert bricklaying below and happily whistling away at the ladies who went by their site. Stan remembers the early days when Albert, in his first office in New Street in Wem, would lie on the floor with exhaustion at the end of a hard days work, working out another quote on the back of a fag packet 'worrying his-self to death and saying as he finished 'Ay that'll do'. At lunchtime Stan would join Albert and Norman Peate and they would go to Ellis's Café in Wem.

In the evenings they would all bicycle home. Ray Grocott, who became the chairman of Gro Continental, would often join them and they would bicycle to 'The Cut' in Whixall.

"Albert was a very good bricklayer. I remember Mr. Gregory's wanted a brick archway built at his house in Wem. There was a lot of hesitation about it so Albert just stood up and got on with it and built a beautiful arch-way that is still there today. He weren't a bad bricklayer!"

When Hill Valley opened Stan became a member. He remembers borrowing his first set of waterproofs from Beryl and buying his first set of clubs in the new Hill Valley pro shop. He has been a member ever since and there is now the Stan Chester Cup.

PAUL HENRY

"I first met Albert in Spain in the early 1980's while playing in a golf competition. He invited me to join his Sparks celebrity charity team and our friendship developed. I used to come to Hill Valley once or twice a year and play golf with Albert and Tony. I was living in Birmingham at the time and they made me an honorary member of Hill Valley. They never could have foreseen that I would come and live here.

In the 1990's I was having fairly substantial difficulties in my personal life and Albert suggested that my wife, Sheila, and I move to Whitchurch. He found us a house and Sheila began working at Hill Valley. Albert, Cyril Forrester and Tony gave me the best help and support in the world and I'm a lot better now than when I arrived here. Things had been bad and they helped pull me through. If it hadn't been for them............ well, they are close to my heart and our friendship has developed as time has gone on. They gave me material help, advice and most of all their company.

They got me away to Spain. I remember Albert in Spain. He would give all the street sellers money but never take their wares. I asked him why and he replied, 'Well they've probably got kids to feed.'

We were playing golf one day in Spain and he suddenly walked away to the side of the course where some builders were laying bricks. He laid a whole course beautifully and enjoyed doing it and having a chat with the men!

Albert, like Cyril Forrester, is of the 'old school'. They are men of their word. They live on the shake of their hand and their word. Everything is done with a handshake and once the deal is said, it's said and they stand by it. They are genuine, it's not an act, just the way they are, men of their word. Albert says things as he sees it but without causing offence and he always acts by his word, the deal and shake of his hand. He never uses his power in a negative way. He'll use it to encourage and talk to every person as an equal.

I've never heard Albert say a bad word about anybody. Even when someone might have pulled a bad stroke against him and he knows it. He's no fool; he's canny and shrewd in business. He might never deal with them again but he will never speak badly of anyone. I think that's a marvellous quality.

And you'd find it difficult to find anyone saying a bad word about him. He's the only man I know who wants to win just the penny on the TV show 'Deal or no Deal' and then he'd give away ten times that to someone who needed it.

There was a young lad once who helped the green keepers but he was struggling to do his part. Albert refused to sack him and he worried about that boy. He would make sure that the lad was fed by Hill Valley at lunch and given his tea too.

People have been coming here year after year, playing golf and loving the great atmosphere. My mates love it; there have never been any airs or graces here at Hill Valley, just good golf and great breakfasts at a good price. Everybody knows Albert and they looked forward to a chat or seeing him out on the course and playing a few holes together. He has great respect in the area and he talks to everybody whoever they are but he can't sit still. He doesn't like hanging around. He was always putting on his golf shoes as he was getting off the plane so as not to waste any time and I'm sure he suffers from a bad stomach because he eats so quickly.

They are and they always will be a big part of my life, even if I left Whitchurch now. Albert, Cyril and Tony pulled me back from bad times; they brought Sheila and I here and we would never leave. I'm a life member now.

Albert and I still play golf and I hope I'm as fit as him at his age. He still plays brilliant golf off a 6 and regularly plays one or two holes although he loves his fishing. As long as nothing interferes with his fishing! He'll never walk away from Hill Valley while he is involved. I think he's enjoyed his life. Incredible man."

ANDY GRIFFITHS

One evening, in the summer of 1972, I was driving my car around Whitchurch with my baby asleep in the back. I drove up to the top of the hill, stopped there and looked down over the land that was to become Hill Valley and saw the fields being transformed. There was very little there but I knew that with Albert's enthusiasm and two of the best course designers, he would do everything right and that in time it would be one of the best courses around.

I first met Albert when I played golf with Tony at Hawkstone as juniors and we became friends. Albert was great at getting all the good young players together and encouraging us to play, and he wouldn't let us pay any green fees. He would take us off to other courses and say, 'You young lads might be good players but you've got to go and play together and play each other on different courses, quality courses'. He meant courses such as Hillside, Birkdale, Lytham St Anne's and Royal St David's. Not only did he then ring them up and book the time for us to go and play but he would say, 'Take my car,' and we would find his brand new Mercedes, full of petrol, waiting for us. We'd drive away, us 17-year-old lads, and Albert wouldn't have a car for the whole day, and he wouldn't let us fill it up on our return.

Then he'd say, 'It's all very well you playing in the summer but you're wasting your time in winter,' so he found out about an African safari golf tour and booked it for three of us, John Anderson, Tony and myself. 'You're all going in January and back in March. Off you go the three of you'. Three young lads and he paid for us! Absolutely amazing. I went in 1973 and

146

again the following year as well. He paid for me twice and then he paid for Woosie to go too.

Albert, Les Welch, Andrew Griffiths and Bob Taylor, wicket keeper for Derbyshire and England.

It wasn't just the finances. He had an older head and he would advise us. He'd find things out that we needed him to find out, that we wouldn't think of finding out for ourselves. He was so enthusiastic for all of us and he sought the best that could be offered or achieved. He took Woosie and all of us out to play. He never pushed us but simply encouraged us; he wanted us all to do well. He was always complimentary and would never put anybody down. 'Try this,' or, 'do that,' and you'll be great,' he would say. Even if someone wasn't a good player he would always suggest something that they could do to make themselves better and build their confidence. Young golfers need people like Albert; he was a brilliant mentor. He gave us opportunities. We all owe him so much.

His encouragement to go and play on championship courses and to go away and play through the winter was great advice at the time. In those days the European Tour stopped from October to the end of March. Now it can take place all year round

147

in countries with warmer climates. Golf academies were available in the mid 1970's in America, but the concept didn't arrive in the UK until many years later. John Garner, a Ryder Cup winner, was one of the first to set up a golf academy in the UK. Albert, always keen to try new ideas, offered him the opportunity to set up an academy and teach at Hill Valley. It was an investment for Albert but money was never the driving force for him. His enthusiasm was a passion to encourage and offer the best for any young golfing talent. The Midland Tournaments were also expensive to host, including the 4 or 5 days loss of green fee revenue, but Albert loved hosting them at Hill Valley. Of course there was press coverage, but it was more than a marketing exercise. I think it was pure fantastic enthusiasm to see how the pro's performed on his course and to be a part of it all.

I became an assistant pro in 1970 at the age of 18 for Wrexham Golf Club. In those days an assistant pro had to have a handicap of 3 or below, take a 12-month assistant pro's course with a fully qualified golf professional and then pass an exam at the end held at Lilleshall Hall.

Those two winters in Nigeria undoubtedly helped my golf and I played in a few tournaments, but essentially I remained a golf professional and not a professional golfer. My golfing career became restricted after I developed a bad neck when I was about 20 years old. It would go into severe spasm for three weeks to a month and then it was always hard to get going again.

I had played 2 rounds in the Canadian PGA when my neck went into spasm again and I felt shattered. After that it was difficult to get back the enthusiasm you need to play golf at that level. I never did want fame; the money would have been nice, but not fame. Looking back now I realise that a big part of the problem was tension, although I wouldn't have admitted it then. I notice even now how easy it is to be tense while playing. With golf the slightest ailment or tinge becomes exaggerated and affects your game. I went to the Augusta Masters with Woosie and there the players had a massage every morning and again straight after play. Playing golf tournaments at that level demands perfect physical and mental condition to play well. I'm full of admiration at how they keep going.

I was happy as the golf professional at Llanymanoch and good links were built between us and Hill Valley. Tony and I ran a joint club week in Majorca taking about 36 members every year for 12 years on a golfing tour.

I was the Welsh champion in 1973 and again in 1980. The first time I won the Midland Pro Tournament was at Hill Valley in the 1980's. I was chuffed to bits that it was at Hill Valley;

that gave me as much pleasure as everything else.

I'm an honorary member of Hill Valley and to play four or five holes with Albert is refreshing because he's still enthusiastic and he'll still trying new things and aiming to get better. He's always got something to talk about. Yet if he doesn't know something, he's not frightened to ask people and learn whatever he can from them. He still regards and treats everyone as an equal, which is lovely to see, because when you've achieved something as he has done, then it's easy for someone to forget himself. He's remained close to his roots and has been marvellous to Shropshire pro's like John Anderson, Jonothan Lomas, Woosie and myself and contributed a lot to where they are today. He's also generous to any golf pro's who visit wherever they come from. He welcomes them with open arms and won't take any green fees from them. Tony also has that quality to talk to anyone and be modest; it's an interest in human nature for its own value.

He loves fishing and he was one of the best fishermen in Shropshire. Many years ago he fished for Shropshire in the All England Championships. He can spend a whole day in his hut very happily. For many years now he's sponsored charity fishing matches for senior citizens at two venues in Staffordshire. His building career was incredible and then he turned to golf and it's been such a big part of his life to play golf.

Albert has inspiration, enthusiasm, generosity, he has a love for life and people and an ability to talk to anybody. I love the story about the elderly couple, who he met on an aeroplane, and then he sent them a cheque to pay for another holiday for them and he didn't want any thanks. That sums him up. Amazing man."

Beryl, Dorothy Kynerston, Albert, Les Welch, Frank Cartwright and Rosie Welch in Tenerife.

Neil Humphries, Tony, Albert, Martin Hall and Bill Smith.

Roger Blake (Captain 1983), Bob Walker, Albert, Les Welch,
Michael Welch, Sandy Lyle and Clive Tinsley.

Cyril and Cath Forrester.

Bill Smith.

Terry Davies, a lifelong friend from Albert's school days.

Val and Shelia Whiston.

Albert with the mayor of Whitchurch Doris Ankers,
September 2007.

17th Tee:

Faith

17th Hole - Par 3 - 175 yards

The shortest of par 3's on the course but some say the toughest; the tee shot into the green requires a long to mid iron with grass bunkers on the left protecting the two tier Mackenzie green which slopes treacherously.

"Albert inspires a sense of peace with others around him."

Tony Hateley

"Plenty of people look happy on the outside but they're crying on the inside."

Albert

An important and constant guiding influence in Albert's life has been his faith.

"Ok, so I am a sinner, not because I may have a nice home or a new car, but because I do not live up to God's standards. He is perfect, I am not, so what can I do about it?

John 1:8 tells me that I should acknowledge it. Jesus tells us in The Bible that He died for sinners like me and that is what I rely on and hope you do too.

All you have to have is faith.

The Devil says, "Face it, you'll never be good enough, why not just give up and accept my way?"

I can tell you from my experience that it would only lead to disaster. We all have choices and you and I need to make the right ones."

"My Christian faith first came from my mother and father and they taught me to go to church. I didn't particularly like going when I was young, I'd rather have gone fishing but by the time I was 12 or 13 years old the girls were prettier which made it easier and it probably did me good in the end. Now I go to a Bible class on a Saturday morning with the 7th Day Adventists and I go to the Methodist church in Whitchurch on a Sunday.

I didn't have a good education but I've studied The Bible and it took me years to understand it. The part that stays with me all the time is, 'seek and you will find'. God will explain it to you and He will answer you. If you don't seek you won't find and it's your loss.

My Christian faith has bought me through many problems and without it I wouldn't have been able to get through them. I was in a desperate state in the early 1960's. Too much drinking and wild living and I sunk to the lowest point in my life. I got on my knees and asked for help. Help came in the twinkling of an eye and I instantly felt like a different person. There are many times in your life when you have to get down on your knees.

Some people do live their lives without any faith at all but I think everybody needs to believe in something or they'll have all manner of problems if they don't. Some people enjoy wealth but I've never found that does any good at all just on its own. All the material things, even the Rolls Royce I bought and I enjoy, are false things really. The pleasure never lasts. Alcohol and drugs are not good either. I don't need any of them; the great thing for me is the Christian faith. Then all of the other wonderful things can follow; the cars or homes or whatever it is that you desire, but I have found they are not the most important things in life. The most important things are to live a life and be friendly to everybody. So I leave other people to think and believe what they want and I get on with my way. There are all manner of faiths and some people believe what they have been taught and some people believe what they have learnt for themselves. I am friendly with people with different faiths. I think everybody is equal. I don't think I've ever changed and I hope I never will change. People tell me I haven't and I hope I never shall. I've met many people who are regarded as very important and most of them are decent people but just a few think they are better than others for some reason but that's life.

I've never been successful in anything I've done where I've thought of it alone. If I ramble along by myself, or think I'm clever with some idea, it's always gone wrong. But then I've said, 'Look, this is beyond me, take charge of me, put me right, then God always has. There's a feeling inside me that if God was guiding it, then it was always successful. I think when you believe in God you can't fail and that's when my successes came. That's how I've lived the last forty years. I did have great faith before but I did things that weren't what He tells you to do.

There is nothing whatever to worry about. We live and when we've gone everything carries on so go out and enjoy what you can. As long as you don't do wrong. If you do wrong then of course it will catch up with you. I do believe we all get what we deserve. Many times I've done silly things and I know I shouldn't be doing them and it's cost me dearly in many ways. It's the same with so many of us. There will always be a day of reckoning. Anything you've done will always catch up with you. I used to be worried about it but I'm not now. I believe that I have been as sinful as most people, maybe more. When you are older you can see all the mistakes you've made in your life. We all get into messes now and again and sometimes it's hard to get out of them. I have sinned and everyone sins. Even if they don't do it they think the sin; no one is all good. We've all got problems and we struggle through life and I may say you have to do the best you can. You have to make judgements at certain times and sometimes we make foolish judgements and I've made many of those so I'm not telling anybody how to live their lives. I'm not perfect, I'm not a preacher and I make no judgements. It's just worked for me and I hope that it will work for you.

I'm relaxed and I can put my head on the pillow and sleep soundly at night and that's the most marvellous thing. It feels right and therefore my faith will always be in God. God answers our prayers. 'Knock and the door will be opened to you'. The devil will always be there and you can always get hurt. The more I read the Bible and seek and look to God the more doors are opened. Jesus showed us how to live, 'If you believe in me, you will have eternal life,' He said.

I want to die well I told the actor Paul Henry, a friend and a member of Hill Valley. 'What do you mean?' he said, laughing, but what I meant was not to be frightened of it and be ready. I've developed a good Christian faith and I'm not frightened of death. When I do get called I will be going to the next stage in eternity. I used to be frightened of death when I was younger.

I found a book once called 'God's Calling' in a antique bookshop for 20 pence and I have enjoyed reading it ever since. I like to pass books on, sometimes sending them to friends all over the world. I also read a three monthly devotional called 'Word for Today'.

I have had lots of people talk to me about going to church, they say they can't go, there embarrassed, they feel they are not good enough. My advice to anyone even contemplating to join a church is go for it, you will meet so many warm and friendly people from all types of background. There is good and bad in all parts of life.

I drive to the lake on the 1st tee and generally have a chat with the ducks and geese whilst they eat out of my hand. If you show love to animals and wildlife, you usually get a good response from them. I talk to god every day of my life come rain or shine, sometimes as I go along in my buggy.

So what's life all about? What's the meaning of it? Perhaps some people never think about it but if anyone wants a joyful life, a successful life, a happy time, then believe and do the best you can."

Albert with his good friends the Hill Valley Senior Section.

18th Tee:

Charity

18th Hole - Par 4 - 401 yards

Play from the tee over water to the generous fairway, the green can be reached with a long to mid iron. This shot is over a pond and through two trees there is also another pond on the right hand side as well as two bunkers on the left so distance control and accuracy are the key. A truly superb finishing hole.

If he read in the local paper that an old lady had been robbed or something like that he'd go and quietly put a bag of coal at her door or maybe money through the letterbox. He would dart in, do the job and leave, just like the Scarlet Pimpernel, always remaining anonymous, wanting to do for others without any reward. He's an unsung hero. He should get an award for what he's done so quietly.'

Peter Condliffe

"He would be a billionaire if he could retrieve all the money he's given away.

Andy Griffiths

Albert gives to charities but prefers much to remain anonymous.

"There are only two people who need to know, me and God."

The Hill Valley Golf Club members run many charity events.

The Annual Christmas Lunch for Senior Citizens is perhaps one of the most popular and certainly most looked forward to event of the year.

Albert began holding an annual Christmas lunch for local senior citizens as far back as 1959 when he was based in Wem, where he would organise and provide a sandwiches luncheon. It has continued every year since 1959, moving to Hill Valley in 1975, developing into the full Christmas menu, still provided for by Albert, expanding tenfold in numbers and served by all the members for all local senior citizens who wish to attend.

On December the 11th, 2006, the Annual Christmas Lunch party was attended by 200 guests.

Albert, Paul Henry, Jamie and Andrew.

46th Annual OAP's Xmas Party

At Macdonald Hill Valley Hotel,
Golf & Country Club

Monday 11th December 2006

You must RSVP to this invitation by the 1st
December 2006 to:

Keith Lowe on **01948 66 0700**
Jamie Minshall on **01948 66 0703**

Arrive for 6:00 - 6:30pm for
complimentary Christmas Dinner
& Entertainment.

**YOU MUST BRING THIS TICKET
WITH YOU!**

JOIN US!

PART FOUR

19th Tee

In The Bar:

Hill Valley-Macdonald's Partnership.

19th Hole - Par 4 - just a few more yards

Play from the car park through the entrance hall into the generous sports bar. From there a long shot is required to the bar where water lies in front. A good shot will find you then comfortably in the lounge seats, a short putt will then find the spot.

"Up until 2005 Hill Valley was Albert Minshall and Albert Minshall was Hill Valley."

Anthony Smith

"You can't book a future at my age."

Albert.

In 1972 the PGA did a survey and there were 700 golf courses in the UK. Today there are about 3000 golf courses with about 2.4 million golfers who on average fall into the 25-54-age bracket. 78% of golfers are members of courses.

In 1973 the money allotted for the entire year to the European Golf Tour was £750.000. Today it is 250,000 million pounds per annum.

In 1960 there were 9 18-hole golf courses in Shropshire. and 3 9-hole courses. Today there are 32 courses in Shropshire and Herefordshire.

With Albert at the helm, Hill Valley has played its part in the great development and success of the game of golf in the UK today.

"We've started building again. It's a new £13.5 million hotel and leisure complex. It's a new era for us at Hill Valley and at three score years and ten I hope to see its completion.

The business partnership with Macdonald's is excellent but of course it's not the same as before for me. I worked for 35 years with good mates and we had a lot of fun. I'll never forget those days. There are so many building rules and regulations now I wouldn't like to be starting out in the building business today.

When we built Hill Valley we built it for pleasure and suddenly it became very hard work. We had to make a living and diversify into things like disco's and a nightclub and I'd like to thank all the local people for their support in those early years."

In 1992 an offer of £10 million was made for Hill Valley.

"But what are we going to do on Monday morning?" asked Albert of his sons.

With consternation Tony thought, ' Has he gone mad?'

"It's not right to have that sort of money," continued Albert.

"Well, we could buy Manchester United." Tony replied hopefully, knowing there were possibly a few shares available at that time.

"But I don't know anything about running football."

"Well, you can learn," said Tony.

Albert refused the offer.

Tony later said to his father, "We've just turned down £10 million and we've got to go back to work now."

'My father was never bothered about money,' Tony reflects and work became increasingly hard. The 1990's saw growing numbers of new hotels with golf courses and Hill Valley Hotel and clubhouse was falling behind needing new investment. Although the golf side of the business was going well, Tony was beginning to lose the energy he had had after nine years of the heavy demands of running the hotel and restaurant.

They began to quietly look for partners but with Albert, who did not want to sell the golf side of Hill Valley, in mind.

MACDONALDS HOTEL GROUP

In 2003 they met with Mr. Donald Macdonald, chairman of the Macdonalds Hotels Group, a man who like Albert enjoys fishing. As they discussed a possible deal for Hill Valley at a meeting in Scotland, Albert turned to Mr. Macdonald and asked him,

"Well, why don't you buy me out completely?"

"No, Albert," he said, "we need you there because you are the one who started it and it wouldn't be right not to have you there."

On November 17th 2003 the deal was completed. Albert sold 50% of the shares of Hill Valley Golf and Country Club to Macdonalds Hotels.

In the last four years, Donald Macdonald and I have had many business meetings, luncheons and dinners together. We share many of the same beliefs and work ethics, and I feel this has enabled us to have a good working and personal relationship.

MACDONALD

HILL VALLEY HOTEL, GOLF & COUNTRY CLUB

GOLF NEWSLETTER

MACDONALD
HILL VALLEY HOTEL
GOLF & COUNTRY CLUB

30 YEARS OF GOLF PAR EXCELLENCE

A LITTLE VISION GOES A LONG WAY. WHEN ALBERT MINSHALL FIRST TEAMED UP WITH GOLFING GREATS PETER ALLIS AND DAVID THOMAS IN THE EARLY 1970S TO CREATE HILL VALLEY GOLF COURSE, HE HAD NO IDEA JUST WHAT HE WAS STARTING.

The club opened in 1975 and has been voted among the top ten courses in the country ever since. In the intervening years, a second course and many more superb facilities have been added making this idyllic corner of the Shropshire countryside a favourite destination for golfers from all over the UK and beyond.

This year, an ambitious £10 million project rolled into action to create a brand new luxury hotel with every modern amenity and provide golfers with simply the finest accommodation and leisure facilities available. Thirty years on, Hill Valley is a stunning leisure retreat on a par with any luxury leisure venue in the world.

LUXURY NEW HOTEL OPENING FROM MARCH

After a £10 million investment, the new 4 star Macdonald Hill Valley Hotel, Golf & Country Club has opened its doors to offer superb accommodation and state-of-the-art facilities - all the ingredients for a perfect sporting break.

Ninety beautifully appointed bedrooms provide relaxing retreats at the end of a long day on the course. The new restaurant adds delicious cuisine in elegant surroundings whilst the bar and lounge areas offer warm and inviting places to celebrate a successful day or drown your sorrows!

WHAT THEY SAY...

"The beautiful Emerald Course at Hill Valley is a real favourite of mine. It's a testing course - full of interest and excitement - and provides new challenges every time."

John Lomas, European Tour player

"This is a wonderful, family-run club that always makes us welcome. The golf is superb and so is the hospitality. Golf doesn't get better than this."

Stan Boardman, comedian

"I take my golf seriously. So do the folks at Hill Valley. The golf team looks after everything. It's all here - two superb courses, beautiful scenery and fabulous after-golf facilities. I love it!"

Dennis Taylor, snooker player

"Hill Valley is my pride and joy. I've spent thirty years creating this unique sporting complex and it remains my family's passion, with the new partnership of Macdonald Hotels the future can only be positive. We hope you'll come along and share the enjoyment with us."

Albert Minshall, Macdonald Hill Valley Director

FOR MORE INFORMATION CALL: **0870 194 2133**

Stan Boardman, Dennis Fell, Martin Fell and Clive Hormby.

Jim Harding, official golf starter and a very good friend of Albert's. Jim looked after all golfers on the first tee and was the only person who was at work before Albert, sometimes here at 5am.

TONY

He is seeing his dream fulfilled, because Hill Valley now has the opportunity to go from strength to strength. It's taken the pressure off us as a family business and it's fulfilling a dream he began in 1972. I've always worked well with my father and it's become my dream to finish it too."

ALBERT

"On most days I come down to Hill Valley and I go over a few things with Tony. Business is hard as you get older but I started it as a dream and I'm not walking away from it until it's finished. Although I haven't agreed with everything that has been done, I think we have made a very good job of the new buildings and all I've added are my own little things because as a builder I see things. I wouldn't do anything I didn't think was right. It's certainly better than the first building that I didn't agree with at all and I certainly won't be altering it again! As for the future, well it's all very nice but whether it'll be successful no one knows. I'm here today, whatever happens tomorrow we'll have to see."

HOPES FOR THE FUTURE

"To keep improving the golf course and looking after the wildlife on the course. Making sure that the geese and our Andrew's ducks are cared for. Three years ago there were three water hens, now there are hundreds. The rabbits are very tame and not frightened at all. It's all to do with love. If you show love to anything it'll always come back to you. Look at these hens about us now. They think it's their place. They don't bother about the golfers. The golfers ask me what about these hens and ducks and seem to enjoy them.

If I hadn't done it, if I'd just stuck to property and not turned to golf I'd have been on the road to making fortunes but when I look back, I can go to sleep at night quite happily. I've worked hard but it's been my dream and I'm not walking away until it's completed and it is coming to completion. Just to finish off this dream, that's my hope for the future."

One wet, cold and windy day in North Shropshire in 2006, Albert in his great coat with a small pencil and a scrap of paper in his hand, stops for a greeting or a chat to everyone he meets and with eagerness waves the scrap of paper in his hand and says, 'We're putting in a driving range and golf academy. I'm designing a little course for the youngsters'. His enthusiasm for Hill Valley is as inspired as it was in 1972 when he bought the land belonging to two farms.

On April 23rd 2006 the new 81-bedroom hotel and function room for about 400 people was opened. Albert greeted the first guests at their evening dinner and was there again to check the first breakfast the next morning. He asked the guests to say what they thought of everything from the bedrooms to the food and to mention any little faults they may have found. Their feedback was good.

"When I look back to thirty years ago when we first opened, how things have changed! It's costing millions. At my age now it doesn't make too much difference and I think it'll be good for the future. How long we stay in it, well, we'll have to see how things go. When you lose control of something, and I've had complete control in my business for all my life, for 50 odd years, I may say it's a difficult position. I'm the sort of person who likes my own way! I've always listened to other people, to their arguments but I have always chosen whether or not to agree and exactly what to do. Now it's not so easy. Now I have to agree with what others do when I might do something differently or spend the money in different ways."

The official opening of the new Macdonald Hill Valley Hotel, Golf and Country Club took place on Monday 9th October 2006. Sandy Lyle, the son of Alex Lyle who had so skilfully encouraged Albert during his earliest golfing days, in affiliation with Macdonald Hotels, launched both the opening of the new hotel and a busy week of golfing and social events.

"Who knows? Nobody knows. I'm very happy with how it's all turned out and hope it continues well. We put it into God's hands."

Psalm 37 Verse 23-24

If the LORD delights in many ways, he makes his step firm; though he stumble he stumble he will not fall, for the LORD uploads him with his hand.

HILL VALLEY GOLF & COUNTRY CLUB

Invites you to our

20th Anniversary Celebration Party

Thursday 29th June 1995

8.30pm for 9.00pm   RSVP by Friday 9th June 1995   Evening Dress

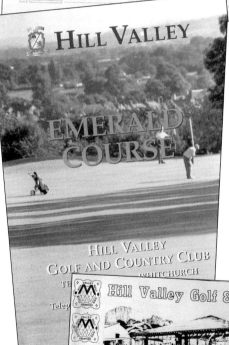

HILL VALLEY

EMERALD COURSE

HILL VALLEY
GOLF AND COUNTRY CLUB
WHITCHURCH

Tele...

Hill Valley
Country Club

Founded   1975

VISITORS BROCHURE

1987

DAILY GOLFERS WELCOME
SOCIETY VISITS . CONFERENCES
BILLIARDS ROOM . SQUASH . SAUNA
FUNCTIONS . PRIVATE PARTIES . WEDDINGS

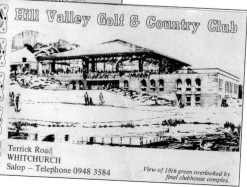

Hill Valley Golf & Country Club

Terrick Road
WHITCHURCH
Salop – Telephone 0948 3584

View of 18th green overlooked by
final clubhouse complex.

167

HILL VALLEY PRESIDENTS, CAPTAINS AND EVENT RECORDS
1975-2006 (compiled by Anthony Smith)

Year	PRESIDENT	CAPTAIN	LADY CAPTAIN	TEAM EVENT	COUNTY CHAMPIONSHIP	COUNTY INDIVIDUAL CHAMPION	NATIONAL SELECTION
1990	Brian Hockenhull	Alan Griffiths	Marianne Hughes	Handicap League	Amateur Junior Open	Michael Welch Michael Welch Kevin Valentine	England Boys (Capt) Michael Welch
1991	Ray Grocott	John Hollinshead	Thelma Windsor	Hargrove Trophy Chronicle Cup Handicap League	Amateur Open	Michael Welch Michael Welch	
1992	Fred Higgs	Bernard Siertsema	Pam Shaw	Handicap League	Amateur Open	Michael Welch Jonathon Lomas	England Youths Michael Welch
1993	"	Walter Heys	Kath Carr		Amateur Senior	Michael Welch Albert Minshall	England
1994	"	Peter Vermeulen	Sue Higgs	Hargrove Trophy	Amateur Senior	Michael Welch Albert Minshall	Michael Welch England Michael Welch
1995	"	"	Phyllis Boughey		Senior	Albert Minshall	Michael Welch
1996	"	Harry Carr	Joyce Buckle	"Mail on Sunday" Runners-Up	(Foursomes)	Rowly Jones & Andrew Minshall	
1997	Albert Murphy	Barry Catterall	Caroline Hocknell	"J Clee Salver" Runners-Up	County President Open	Anthony Smith Tony Minshall	
1998	"	Mike Teates	Rosie Booth	Hargrove Trophy Scratch League	Midland Seniors Senior	Anthony Smith Anthony Smith	
1999	"	Andrew Minshall	Joyce Reeves	Scratch League Matchplay	County President Matchplay Senior	Carl Ciesielski Anthony Smith Andrew Minshall	
2000	"	Norman Buckle	Wendy Bartlett	Scratch League Handicap League	Matchplay Midland Seniors Team	Albert Minshall & Anthony Smith	
2001	"	Stan Hopley	Beryl Young	Scratch League	Senior	Anthony Smith	England Seniors Anthony Smith
2002	"	Garry Bailey	Maura Murphy	Hargrove Trophy Handicap League	Senior	Anthony Smith	England Seniors Anthony Smith
2003	Harry Carr	Keith Moulton	Sue De Barro	Hargrove Trophy Handicap League	Senior	Anthony Smith	England Seniors Anthony Smith
2004	"	Dennis Clutton	Gwen Thomas	Handicap League	Senior	Anthony Smith	England Seniors Anthony Smith
2005	"	Peter Willmouth	Pat Brown				
2006	Anthony Smith	Fred Higgs	Maura Murphy				

HILL VALLEY Records since 1975

YEAR	PRESIDENT	CAPTAIN	LADY CAPTAIN	COUNTY TEAM EVENT	COUNTY CHAMPIONSHIP	COUNTY INDIVIDUAL CHAMPION	NATIONAL SELECTION
1976	Geoff Fox	John Davies	Margaret Hiles	Handicap League			
1977	"	George Ashworth		Junior League	Amateur Open	Anthony Smith Ian Woosnam	
1978	John Edwards	Oscar Williams	Mary Wise		Open Matchplay	Anthony Smith Ian Woosnam	
1979	Frank Davies	Brian Hockenhull	Babs Jones	Handicap League	Amateur Open	Anthony Smith Tony Minshall	
1980	Tom Williams	Huw Griffith	Doreen Osborne	Junior League	Amateur Open	Anthony Smith Tony Minshall	
1981	Richard Latham	Ray Grocott	Anne Timperley	Junior League	Open	Tony Minshall	
1982	"	Albert Murphy	Nina Hanlin	Hargrove Trophy Handicap League	Matchplay Open Junior	John Williams Tony Minshall Andrew Hall	
1983	Brian Hockenhull	Roger Blake	Irene Clay	Handicap League	Open J Clee Salver (Foursomes)	Tony Minshall Kevin Valentine & John Williams	
1984	"	Les Boughey	Mary Done	Handicap League	J Clee Salver (Foursomes) Open	Andrew Hall & Nick Minshall Tony Minshall	
1985	"	Frank Davies	Margaret Barnett	Handicap League	Junior J Clee Salver (Foursomes)	Duncan Hall Anthony Smith & Kevin Valentine	
1986	"	John Bellis	Jean Poole	Handicap League			
1987	"	John Pickering	Brenda Sientsema				
1988	"	Graham Buckle	Madge Woollam				
1989	"	Clive Jones	Shirley Johnson		Amateur Junior J Clee Salver (Foursomes)	Michael Welch Michael Welch Nigel Chesters & Michael Welch	England Boys Michael Welch

THE CUPS AND TROPHIES OF
HILL VALLEY GOLF CLUB

THE MENS' CUPS

Club Championship:
Donated by Albert Minshall and Les Welch. Albert donates all the prizes annually.

Peter Alliss Trophy:
Donated by Peter Alliss, co designer of the course.

WH Smith Salver:
Donated by M. Anthony Smith of WH Smith's Foundry in Whitchurch.

B. Hockenhull Seniors Trophy:
Donated by Brian Hockenhull. Captain in 1979 and President from 1984- 1990.

The Brittania Aggregate Trophy:
Donated by the Brittania Building Society

Seniors' Match play Trophy:
Donated by Alan Griffiths, Captain in 1990.

J.Forster Jubilee Trophy:
Donated by john Forster, a local businessman in scaffolding.

Old Cyril Cup:
Donated by Albert Minshall in memory of Cyril Edge, who worked for many years at Hill Valley and was renowned for his bunker raking.

J. Hockenhull Easter Cup:
Donated by Joan Hockenhull, wife of the late Brian.

Emerald Winter League Cup:
Donated by Conrad Elson.

NH and J. Peake Cup:
Donated by friends of Albert Minshall.

Herald Rose Bowl:
Donated by the local newspaper: The Whitchurch Herald.

S. Chester's Cup:
Donated by Stan Chester, founder member and local builder.

Rabbits Cup:
Anonymous donation from a Hill Valley member.

President's Putter:
Donated by Brian Hockenhull in 1983.

Captain's Driver:
Donated by John Pickering in 1987.

Wem Motor Services Veterans' Cup:
Donated by an old friend of Albert's, Wilf Birch.

Walter Heys Seniors' Trophy:
Donated by Walter Heys.

THE LADIES CUPS

Ladies' Club Championship:
Donated by Neville Shaw and Pam Shaw
(Ladies Captain 1992)

Stella Dodd Rose Bowl:
Donated by Stella Dodd, an original member.

Menwall Designs Cup:
Donated by Mike Shuiker an original member.

Bill Smith cup:
Donated by Bill Smith, a local builder and close friend
of Albert's.

Harry Carr Easter cup:
Donated by Harry Carr an original member
(Captain 1996. President 2003-2005)

Babs Jones Silver Trophy:
Donated by Babs Jones, secretary (multi-tasked) for Albert.

Brenda Siertsema Trophy:
Donated by Brenda Siertsema.

Clewlow Greensome:
Donated by Edna and Julie Clewlow.

Emma Cawkwell Trophy:
Donated as the trophy for a tournament for players with a handicap of 36, lowered in the mid 1980's to 30.

Brenda Garside Trophy:
Donated by Brenda Garside for the winner of the Stableford competition.

Anne Timperley Cup:
Donated by Anne Timperley. A competition for the eight ladies with the four best aggregate scores in a year.

THE MIXED CUPS

Mary and Frank Johnson Cup:
Donated by Mary and Frank Johnson

Bateman Salvers:
Donated by Harold and Phyllis Bateman who owned the farmland Albert bought to build Hill Valley golf course.

Les and Rose Welch Cup:
Donated by Les and Rose Welch. Les was Albert's business partner.

A.J. and B. Minshall Cup:
Donated by Albert and Beryl Minshall.

Albert Murphy Memorial Trophy:
Donated by Mrs A.P. Murphy, Maura (Lady Captain in 2002) in memory of her husband Albert Murphy who was Captain in 1982 and president from 1997-2002.

Jenny Valentine Memorial:
Donated by the Valentine family. Kevin and Colin were both junior members. Kevin became a professional at Hill Valley and Mrs Valentine was a keen supporter of the junior section.

Jim Harding Cup:
Donated by Ruth Harding in memory of Jim who was the starter at Hill Valley.

Malcolm Goodwin Trophy:
Donated as a memorial trophy for Malcolm Goodwin.

THE SAPPHIRE COURSE TROPHIES

The Frostbite Trophy:
Instigated by the Sapphire committee of 1997-1998 as a winter competition starting in January. First held in 1998

Sue and Fred Higgs Trophy:
Donated by Fred Higgs (President 1992-1996)

Sue Tole Greensome:
Donated by Sue Tole. Two trophies for pairs.

'93 Salver:
Donated by the Sapphire committee of 1993.

Bogey Trophy:
Suggested by a lady member where Individuals play against their own card and the course rather than against an opponent.

Turkey Trots:
A competition held in Decamber with a turkey as the prize.

Easter Stableford:
Played in April with a trophy donated by the committee.

Birdie Competition:
A prize, which used to be a Beswick bird, donated by Mary Stockton for the female player with the highest score of birdies in one year.

JANUARY

Date	Event	Course
Sun.1st	Captains' Drive-In	Emerald
Sat.7th	LGU Medal	Emerald
Mon.9th	LGU Medal	Emerald
Sun.15th	Frostbite Trophy	Sapphire
Sat.21st	Stableford	Emerald
Sun.22nd	Texas Scramble (Mixed)	Emerald
Mon.23rd	Stableford	Emerald

FEBRUARY

Date	Event	Course
Sat.4th	LGU Medal	Emerald
Mon.6th	LGU Medal	Emerald
Sat.18th	Stableford	Emerald
Mon.20th	Stableford	Emerald
Sun.26th	LGU Medal	Sapphire

MARCH

Date	Event	Course
Thurs.2nd	LGU Medal	Sapphire
Sat.4th	LGU Extra Medal	Emerald
Sun.5th	Trio Competition (Lady/Gent/Junior)	Emerald
Mon.6th	LGU Extra Medal	Emerald
Sun.12th	Mixed Greensome	Sapphire
Mon.13th	Ladies' Luncheon (Back 9 Holes)	Emerald
Sat.18th	Stableford	Emerald
Mon.20th	Stableford	Emerald

APRIL

Date	Event	Course
Sat.1st	LGU Medal	Emerald
Sun.2nd	Jenny Valentine Trophy (Mixed)	Emerald
Mon.3rd	LGU Medal	Emerald
Sat.8th	Friendly v Llangollen (Mixed-Home)	Emerald
Wed.12th	Coronation Foursomes	Emerald

APRIL CONT'D...

Date	Event	Course
Mon.17th	Harry Carr Easter Cup	Emerald
Thurs.20th	Easter Stableford	Sapphire
Fri.21st	Friendly v Delamere (Home)	Emerald
Sat.22nd	Stableford	Emerald
Mon.24th	Stableford	Emerald
Sun.18th	LGU Extra Medal	Emerald
Fri.28th	Ladies v Gents	Emerald
Sat.29th	LGU Extra Medal	Emerald
Sun.30th	F & M Johnson Cup (Mixed)	Emerald

MAY

Date	Event	Course
Mon.1st	LGU Extra Medal	Emerald
Wed.3rd	Ping 4BBB Tournament	Emerald
Mon.8th	Charity Texas Scramble	Emerald
Wed.10th	Friendly v Brookfield (Away)	Emerald
Sat.13th	Stableford	Emerald
Mon.15th	Stableford	Emerald
Wed.17th	League v Llanymynech (Away)	Sapphire
Thurs.18th	Sue & Fred Higgs Trophy	Sapphire
Mon.22nd	Emma Cawkwell Trophy	Emerald
Thurs.25th	League v Mile End (Home)	Emerald
Sat.27th	Friendly v Upton (Mixed-Home)	Emerald
Sun.28th	Stableford	Sapphire
Mon.29th	Mixed Open Greensome	Emerald

JUNE

Date	Event	Course
Thurs.1st	Stableford	Sapphire
Fri.2nd	Friendly v Wrexham (Home)	Emerald
Sat.3rd	LGU Extra Medal	Emerald
Sat.29th	Captain's Day	Emerald
Sun.4th	LGU Extra Medal	Emerald

JUNE CONT'D...

Date	Event	Course
Wed.7th	Ladies' Open	Emerald
Sat.10th	LGU Medal & Ritchie Salver	Sapphire
Mon.12th	LGU Medal & Ritchie Salver	Emerald
Wed.14th	Senior Ladies' Salver	Emerald
Sat.17th	Stableford	Emerald
Sun.18th	LGU Extra Medal	Sapphire
Mon.19th	Stableford	Emerald
Wed.21st	League v Llanymynech (Home)	Emerald
Thurs.22nd	LGU Extra Medal	Sapphire
Mon.26th	Lady Captain's Day	Emerald
Wed.28th	Clewlow Greensome	Emerald
Thurs.29th	LGU Medal	Sapphire

JULY

Date	Event	Course
Sun.2nd	Jim Harding Memorial Trophy (Mixed)	Emerald
Sun.2nd	LGU Medal	Sapphire
Mon.3rd	Lady Captain's Trophy (B Siertsema)	Emerald
Wed.5th	Menwal Designs Cup	Emerald
Sun.9th	President's Day	Emerald
Mon.10th	Stella Dodd Rose Bowl (Round 1)	Emerald
Wed.12th	Stella Dodd Rose Bowl (Round 2)	Emerald
Sat.15th	LGU Medal	Emerald
Sun.16th	LGU Medal	Sapphire
Mon.17th	Stableford	Emerald
Thurs.20th	Stableford	Emerald
Sun.23rd	A Murphy Memorial Trophy (Mixed)	Sapphire
Wed.26th	Ladies' Invitation	Emerald
Fri.28th	Friendly v Shrewsbury (Home)	Emerald
Sat.29th	Mixed Friendly v Upton (Away)	Emerald
Mon.31st	LGU Medal	Emerald

HILL VALLEY GOLF CLUB

LADIES' FIXTURE LIST 2006

Captain:	Maura Murphy
Vice Captain:	Sarah McGinley
Hon. Secretary:	Moira Pearson
Competition Secretary:	Gwen Thomas
Handicap Secretary:	Sue DeBarro

AUGUST

Date	Event	Venue
Wed 2nd	Past Captains' Trophy	Emerald
Sun 6th	Stableford	Sapphire
Mon 7th	Babs Jones Silver Trophy	Emerald
Thurs 10th	Stableford	Sapphire
Mon 14th	Brenda Garside Trophy	Emerald
Mon 21st	Medal Winners' Trophy	Emerald
Thurs 24th	Captain v Vice Captain	S & E
Sat 26th	LGU Extra Medal	Emerald
Mon 28th	LGU Extra Medal	Emerald
Wed 30th	Friendly v Llangollen (Home)	Emerald

SEPTEMBER

Date	Event	Venue
Sat 2nd	A) & B Minshull Cup (Mixed)	Emerald
Mon 4th	LGU Medal & Pendant	Emerald
Thurs 7th	Sue Tole Greensome	Sapphire
Sat 9th	LGU Medal & Pendant	Emerald
Sat 9th	Friendly v Llangollen (Mixed – Away)	....
Sun 10th	Bateman Salver (Mixed)	Emerald
Mon 11th	Anne Timperley Cup	Emerald
Mon 18th	Stableford & Motor Neurone	Emerald
Sat 23rd	Stableford & Motor Neurone	Emerald
Sat 23rd	Friendly v Hawkstone (Mixed-Home)	Emerald
Mon 25th	Charity Texas Scramble	Emerald
Thurs 28th	Bogey Competition	Sapphire
Sat 30th	LGU Medal	Emerald
	Texas Scramble v Upton (Away)	....

OCTOBER

Date	Event	Venue
Sun 1st	Malcolm Goodwin (Mixed)	Sapphire
Mon 2nd	LGU Medal	Emerald
Thurs 5th	Friendly v Hawkstone (Away)	....
Sun 8th	Stableford	Sapphire

OCTOBER CONT'D...

Date	Event	Venue
Mon 9th	Daily Mail Foursomes	Emerald
Thurs 12th	Stableford	Sapphire
Sat 14th	LGU Extra Medal	Emerald
Sun 15th	Texas Scramble (Mixed)	Emerald
Mon 16th	LGU Extra Medal	Emerald
Mon 23rd	Ladies Annual Dinner	
Thurs 26th	'93 Salver	Sapphire

NOVEMBER

Date	Event	Venue
Sun 5th	Stableford	Sapphire
Mon 6th	Ladies' AGM	....
Thurs 9th	Club Annual Dinner	Sapphire
Fri 10th	Turkey Trot (15 Holes)	Emerald
Sat 11th	LGU Medal	Emerald
Thurs 16th	Turkey Trot (15 Holes)	Sapphire
Sat 18th	Stableford	Emerald
Sun 19th	Turkey Trot (Mixed-15 Holes)	Emerald
Mon 20th	Stableford	Emerald
Mon 20th	Club AGM	....
Mon 27th	Turkey Trot (15 Holes)	Emerald

DECEMBER

Date	Event	Venue
Sat 2nd	LGU Medal	Emerald
Sun 3rd	Texas Scramble (Mixed)	Sapphire
Mon 4th	LGU Medal	Emerald
Sat 9th	Stableford	Emerald
Mon 11th	Stableford	Emerald
Thurs 14th	Christmas Bring & Win	Emerald
Sun 17th	Christmas Spirits (Mixed-15 Holes)	Sapphire
	Prize Presentation	Emerald

Emerald Course
Aerial view
1980's

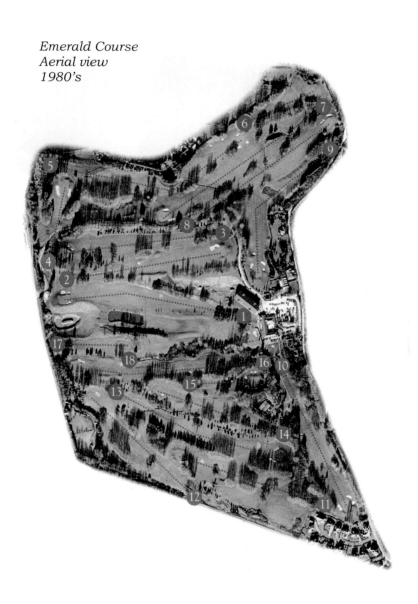

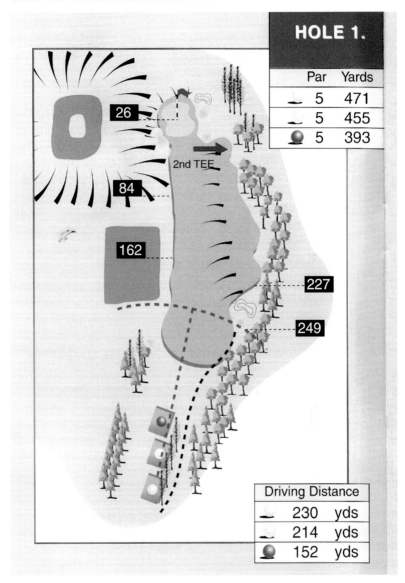

HOLE 1.

	Par	Yards
	5	471
	5	455
	5	393

Labels on map: 26, 84, 162, 227, 249, 2nd TEE

Driving Distance		
	230	yds
	214	yds
	152	yds

1st Hole - Par 5 - 471 yards

An inviting tee shot just the fairway bunker on the right to avoid on the otherwise generous fairway. A good tee shot will leave a fairway wood or long iron in to the long green protected by three large greenside bunkers and a pond to the lower right hand side of the green, a good hole to pick up a birdie on.

177

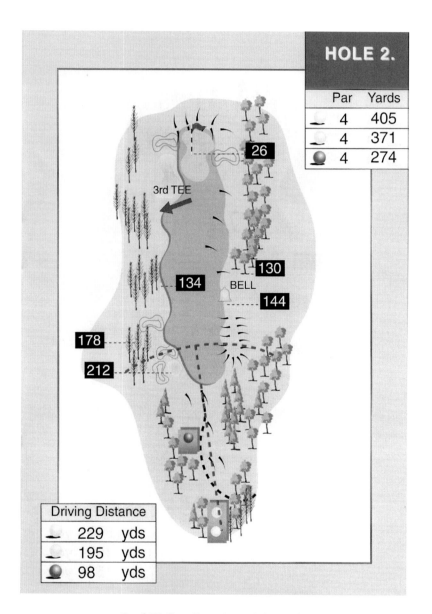

3rd TEE

26

130

134

BELL

144

178

212

Driving Distance		
	229	yds
	195	yds
	98	yds

2nd Hole - Par 4 - 405 yards

Blind tee shot over the crest of the hill with a dominant oak tree hounding the left hand side of the fairway, but don't leak the shot off to the right as the fairway falls away over a mound into trees. Once the fairway is found a mid to long iron should find the back to front sloping green with a large bunker wrapped around the left hand side.

178

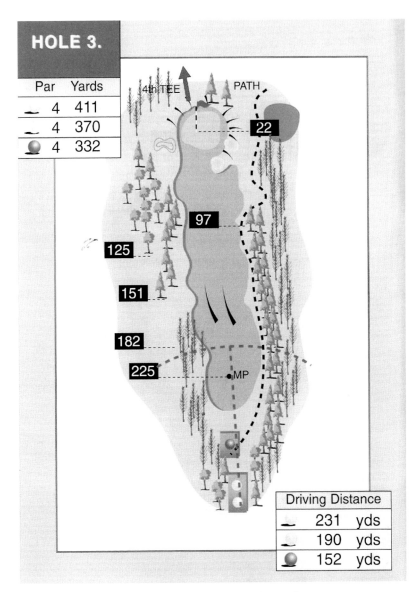

HOLE 3.

Par	Yards
4	411
4	370
4	332

4th TEE

PATH

22

97

125

151

182

225

MP

Driving Distance		
	231	yds
	190	yds
	152	yds

3rd Hole - Par 4 - 411 yards

Tee off over the crest of the hill to a large fairway the better player will hit a fairway wood off the tee and try and hug the right hand side of the fairway for a better approach to the green. A mid to short iron should be a comfortable choice into the Plateau green protected by two pot bunkers at the front and fierce slopes at the rear.

179

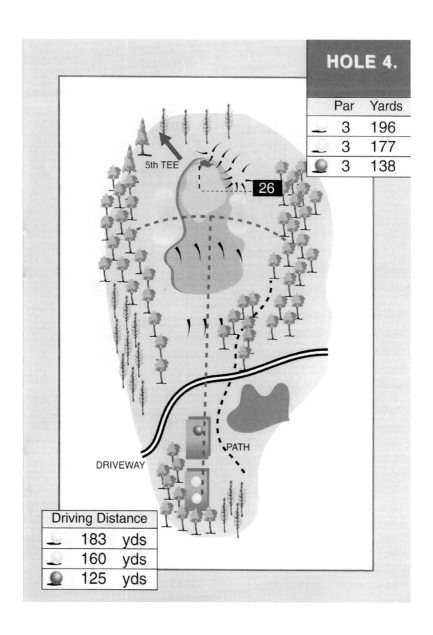

HOLE 4.

Par	Yards
3	196
3	177
3	138

Driving Distance

183	yds
160	yds
125	yds

5th TEE

26

PATH

DRIVEWAY

4th Hole - Par 3 - 196 yards

An uphill demanding par 3 that even the best of players hit a long iron into with a long green protected by two large bunkers either side.

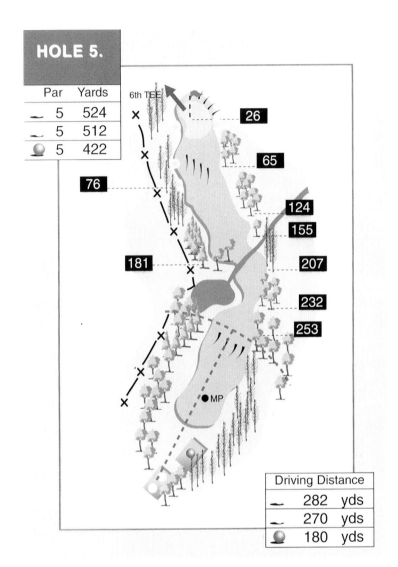

HOLE 5.

Par	Yards
5	524
5	512
5	422

6th TEE

26

65

76

124

155

181

207

232

253

MP

Driving Distance		
	282	yds
	270	yds
	180	yds

5th Hole - Par 5 - 524 yards

The most demanding of par 5's on the course, a tee shot over
the crest of the hill in to a generous fairway, but precision of
the shot is imperative as the second shot over the pond is defended by poplar trees on the right and left hand sides. Most
players usually hit a long iron to lay up on the right hand side
of the fairway. Three bunkers protect the green which slopes
fiercely from front to back and putts from the back of the green
have to be treated with the utmost care.

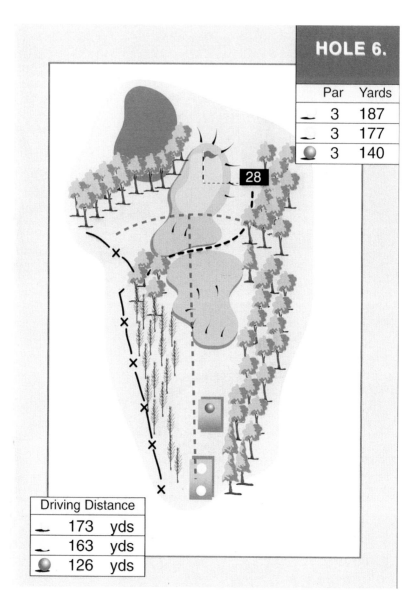

	Par	Yards
—	3	187
—	3	177
●	3	140

28

Driving Distance		
—	173	yds
—	163	yds
●	126	yds

6th Hole - Par 3 - 187 yards

From the tee only the right side of the green can be seen at 187 yards a mid to long iron is the club but don't pull the shot to left as water behind the green protects the hole from the over ambitious player, also be wary of the road that runs in front of the green.

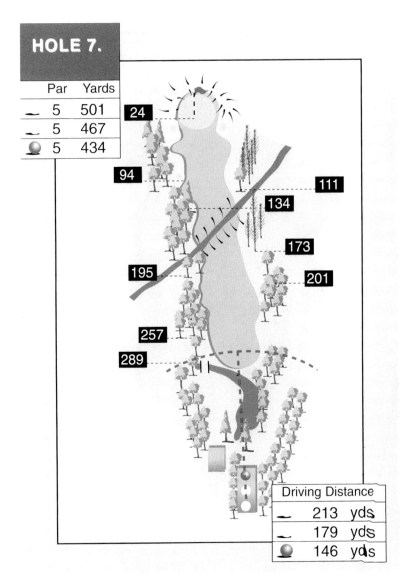

HOLE 7.

	Par	Yards
—	5	501
—	5	467
⦿	5	434

24

94

111

134

173

195

201

257

289

Driving Distance		
—	213	yds
—	179	yds
⦿	146	yds

7th Hole - Par 5 - 501 yards

The tee shot here requires you to carry the ball over two streams onto the fairway guarded both left and right by trees. Players will then attack the green over another stream with a fairway bunker on the right hand side. The better player will take the green on in two but with a bunker on the left hand side and another on the right wrapping round to the front of the green the entrance is quite tight.

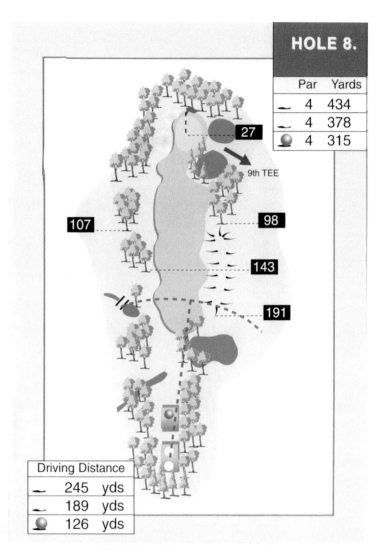

HOLE 8.

	Par	Yards
—	4	434
—	4	378
⬤	4	315

27

9th TEE

107

98

143

191

Driving Distance		
—	245	yds
—	189	yds
⬤	126	yds

8th Hole - Par 4 - 434 yards

Stroke index 1 on the card and arguably one of the toughest par 4's around. Tee off from the slightly elevated tee and thread the ball between water on both sides of the fairway but too far left and the second shot becomes blocked out by the dominant oak tree. Once on the fairway the second shot with a mid to long iron is over a pond that stretches from the front of the green completely round the right hand side, further danger lies on the left with two treacherous deep bunkers. If you leave over the buckle bridge here with a par you will have done well.

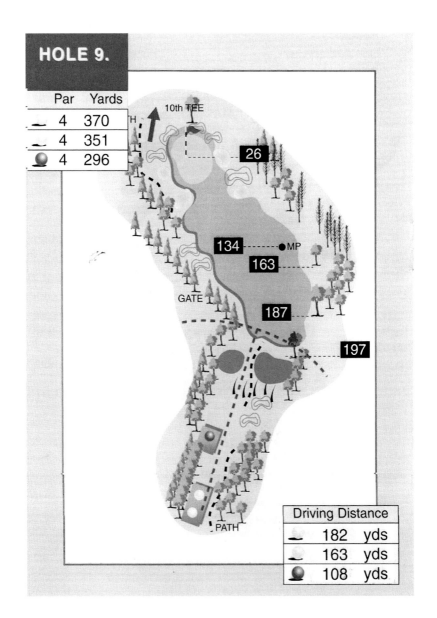

HOLE 9.

Par	Yards
4	370
4	351
4	296

10th TEE

26

134 ---- MP

163

GATE

187

197

Driving Distance		
	182	yds
	163	yds
	108	yds

PATH

9th Hole - Par 4 - 370 yards

A ninety degree dogleg left with out of bounds following the hole down the left hand side. The more aggressive player will attack the corner leaving a short iron in to the green, mere mortals will play straight at the marker hitting a mid iron into the green defended by bunkers on both sides.

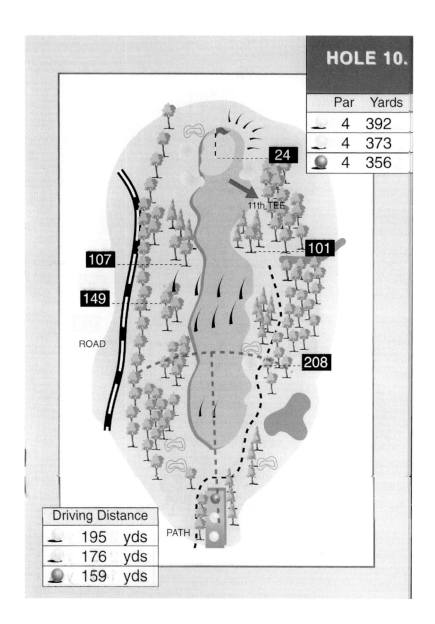

Par	Yards
4	392
4	373
4	356

24

11th TEE

101

107

149

ROAD

208

Driving Distance		
195	yds
176	yds
159	yds

PATH

10th Hole - Par 4 - 392 yards

The tee shot here requires you to thread the ball safely between the oak tree on the right and willow tree on the left. The fairway falls away in front of you in to a small valley. The second shot will just require a short iron into a generous green with bunkers either side.

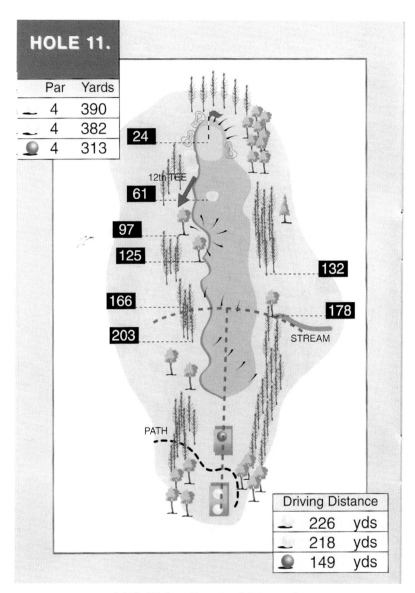

HOLE 11.

Par	Yards
4	390
4	382
4	313

24

12th TEE

61

97

125

132

166

178

203

STREAM

PATH

Driving Distance	
226	yds
218	yds
149	yds

11th Hole - Par 4 - 390 yards

On the tee you can see the fairway in front of you but at driver distance there lies a hollow in the fairway, hit too far and play from there completely blind to the hole. Most players lay short with a fairway wood hitting a mid to short iron into the green. Danger lies on the left hand side with a large bunker gathering wayward shots.

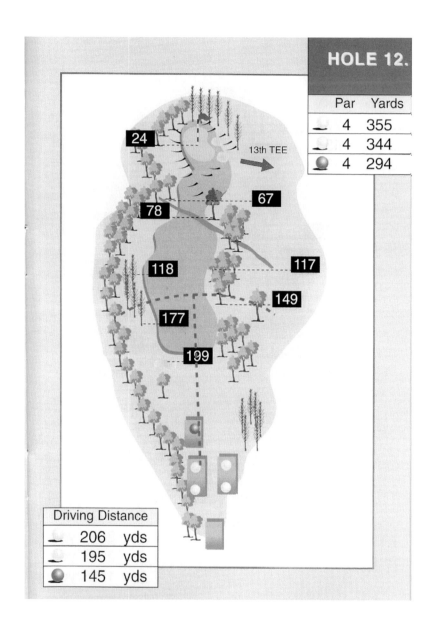

HOLE 12.

	Par	Yards
	4	355
	4	344
	4	294

24

13th TEE

67

78

118

117

149

177

199

Driving Distance		
	206	yds
	195	yds
	145	yds

12th Hole - Par 4 - 355 yards

A blind tee shot over the top of the bank with trees tight either side. The sensible play is to lay up short of the two oak trees, the green is set slightly elevated from the fairway with two bunkers at the back but fall short to the left and the chip shot up to the green is tough.

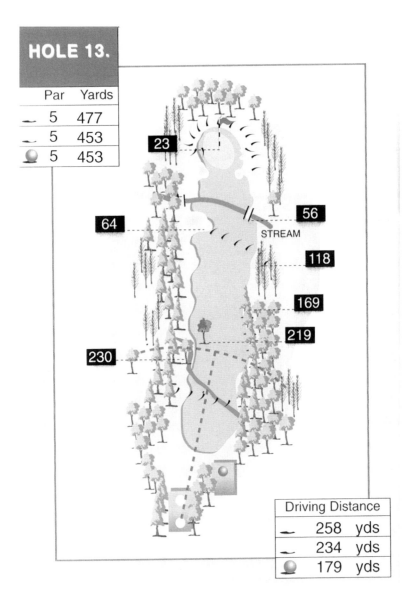

HOLE 13.

	Par	Yards
—	5	477
—	5	453
●	5	453

23

64

56

STREAM

118

169

219

230

Driving Distance		
—	258	yds
—	234	yds
●	179	yds

13th Hole - Par 5 - 477 yards

The easiest of the par 5 holes on the course but still holds its own. The tee shot requires the ball to be hit down the right hand side of the fairway at what the members call the goal posts (two oak trees) as the fairway slopes from left to right towards the line of conifer trees. The green may be within range in two but a stream 20 yards short collects those that don't make it. pot bunkers either side of the green collect way ward shots.

189

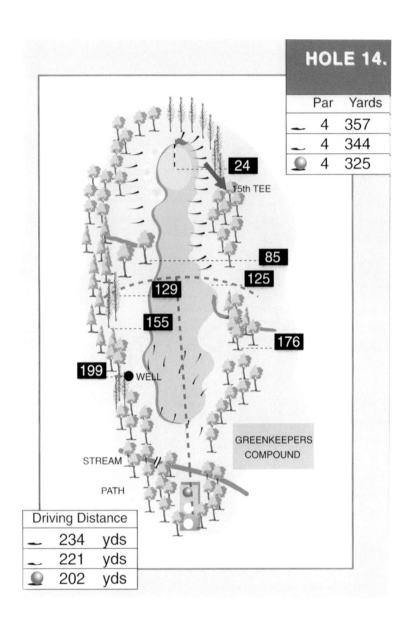

Par	Yards
4	357
4	344
4	325

24

15th TEE

85

125

129

155

176

199 • WELL

GREENKEEPERS
COMPOUND

STREAM

PATH

Driving Distance		
234	yds
221	yds
202	yds

14th Hole - Par 4 - 357 yards

If down the wind the pro's can drive the green here but sensibly lay up short of the tree on the left and miss the ditch on the right leaving a short iron in to the green, this looks quite flat but local knowledge says there is a severe slope from right to left.

HOLE 15.

Par	Yards
3	178
3	146
3	134

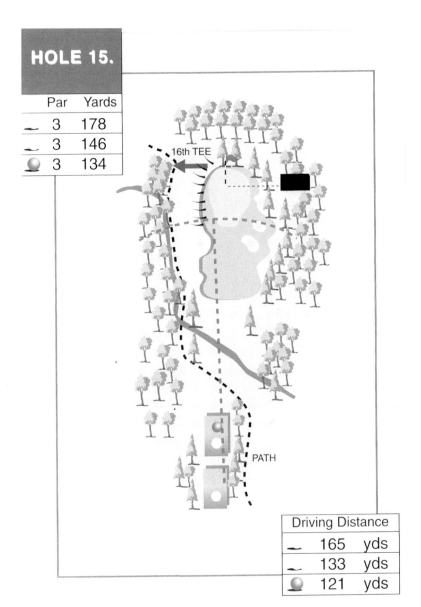

16th TEE

PATH

Driving Distance		
165	yds	
133	yds	
121	yds	

15th Hole - Par 3 - 178 yards

Standing on the elevated tee the tee shot is quite tight to what
looks a simple large target, miss the green either side and one
of the five depp bunkers will collect the ball.

191

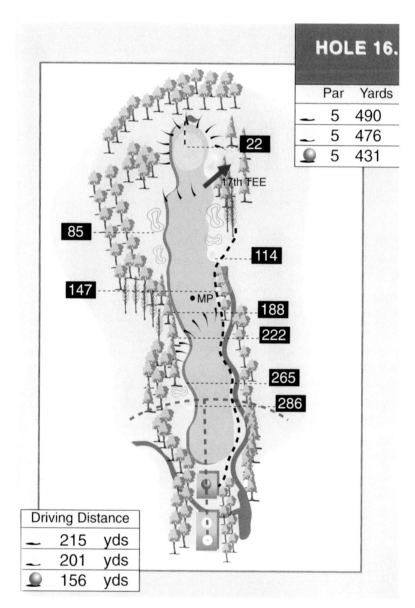

	Par	Yards
—	5	490
—	5	476
●	5	431

22

85

114

147

•MP

188

222

265

286

17th TEE

Driving Distance		
—	215	yds
—	201	yds
●	156	yds

16th Hole - Par 5 - 490 yards

The key to the hole is the tee shot. A tight fairway is protected by the fairway bunker on the left and a lake stretching up the right hand side find the fairway and the second shot is played to the green over the elevated fairway. A fairway wood or long iron should be the club, the bunker on the right collects wayward shots.

HOLE 17.

Par	Yards
3	175
3	152
3	136

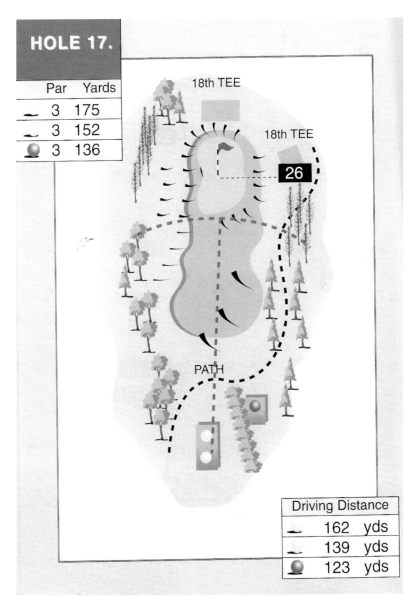

18th TEE

18th TEE

26

PATH

Driving Distance		
162	yds
139	yds
123	yds

17th Hole - Par 3 - 175 yards

The shortest of par 3's on the course but some say the toughest; the tee shot into the green requires a long to mid iron with grass bunkers on the left protecting the two tier Mackenzie green which slopes treacherously.

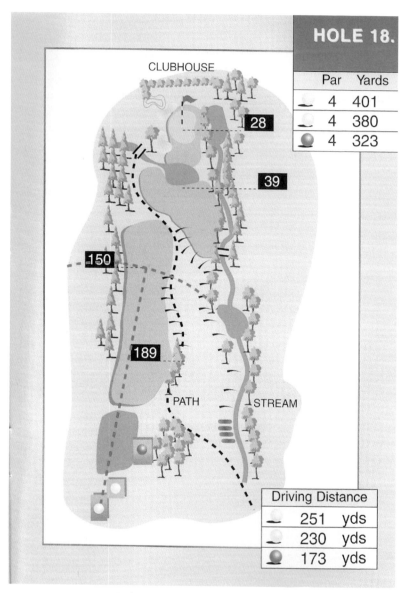

Par	Yards
4	401
4	380
4	323

CLUBHOUSE

28

39

150

189

PATH   STREAM

Driving Distance		
251	yds
230	yds
173	yds

18th Hole - Par 4 - 401 yards

Play from the tee over water to the generous fairway, the green can be reached with a long to mid iron. This shot is over a pond and through two trees there is also another pond on the right hand side as well as two bunkers on the left so distance control and accuracy are the key. A truly superb finishing hole.

19th Hole - Par 4 - Just a few more yards

Play from the car park through the entrance hall into the generous sports bar. From there a long shot is required to the bar where water lies in front. A good shot will find you then comfortably in the lounge seats, a short putt will then find the spot.

Aerial view of Sapphire
Course 1980's

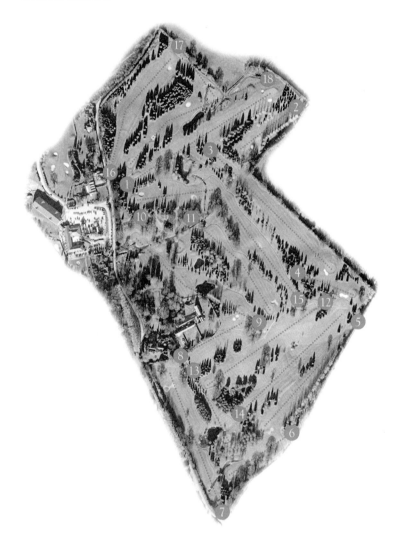

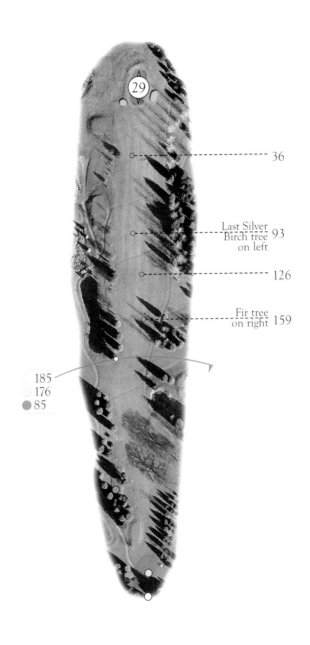

29

36

Last Silver
Birch tree 93
on left

126

Fir tree 159
on right

185
176
85

1st Hole - Par 4 - 388 yards

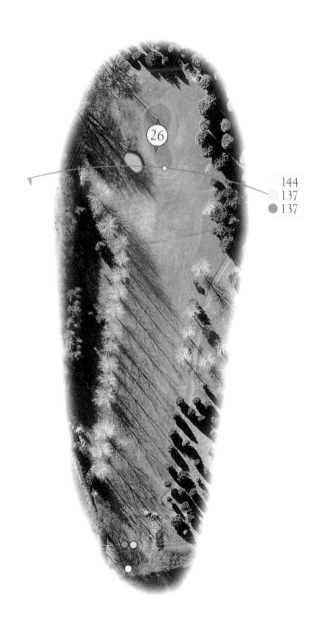

144
137
137

2nd Hole - Par 3 - 157 yards

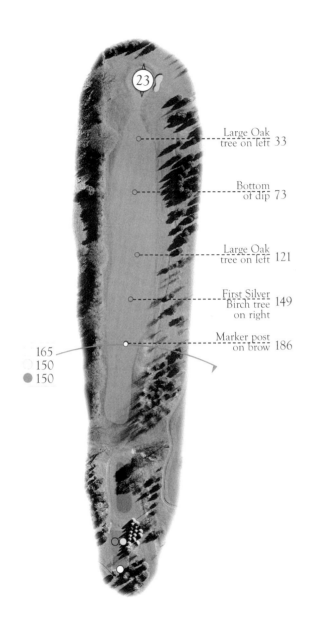

Large Oak
tree on left 33

Bottom
of dip 73

Large Oak
tree on left 121

First Silver
Birch tree 149
on right

Marker post
on brow 186

165
150
150

3rd Hole - Par 4 - 360 yards

199

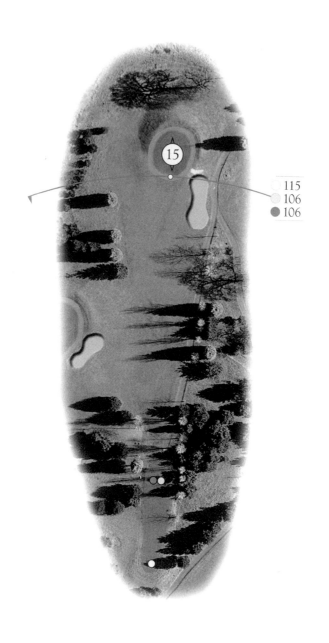

4th Hole - Par 3 - 123 yards

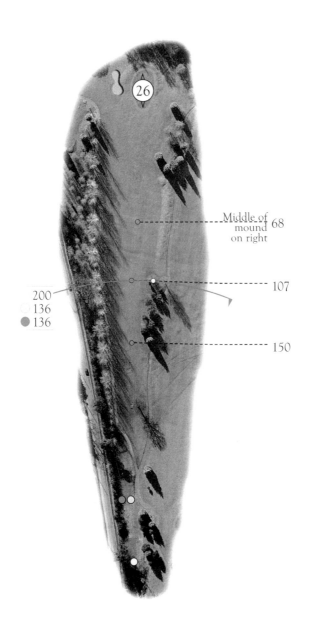

5th Hole - Par 4 - 326 yards

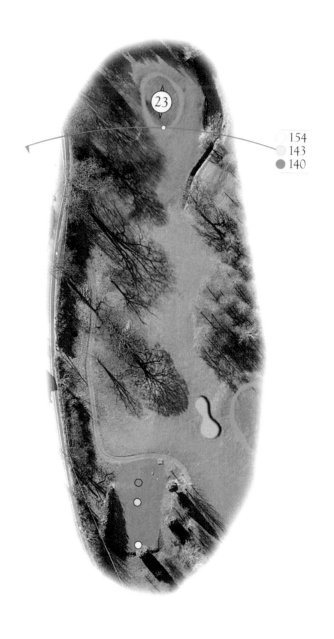

23

154
143
140

6th Hole - Par 3 - 166 yards

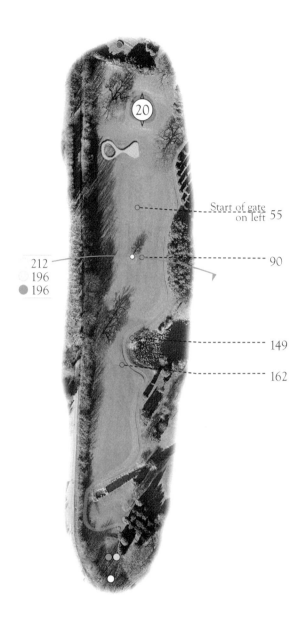

Start of gate
on left 55

212
196
196

90

149

162

7th Hole - Par 4 - 314 yards

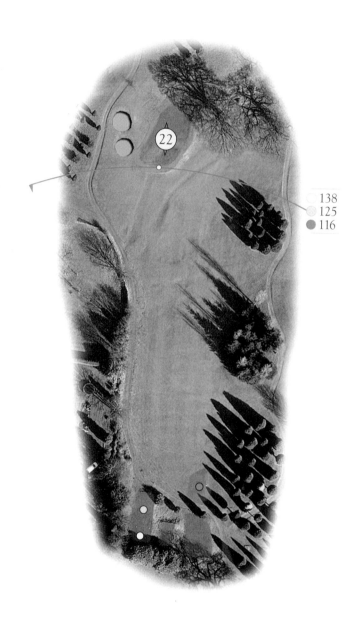

8th Hole - Par 3 - 149 yards

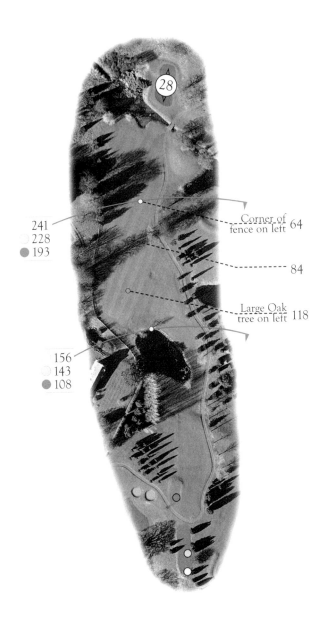

241
228
193

Corner of
fence on left 64

84

Large Oak
tree on left 118

156
143
108

9th Hole - Par 4 - 323 yards

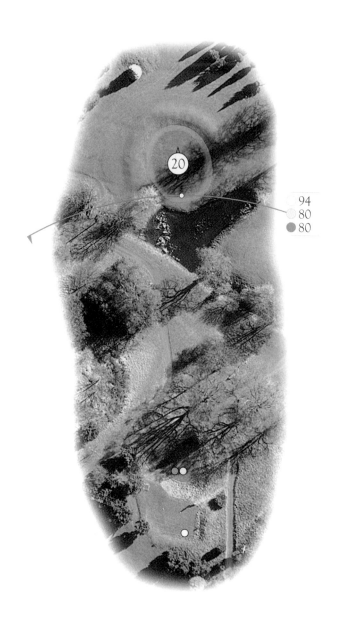

10th Hole - Par 3 - 104 yards

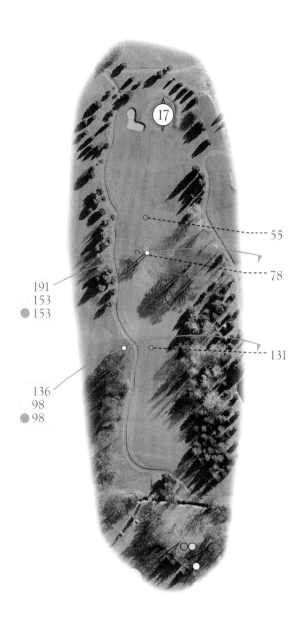

11th Hole - Par 4 - 288 yards

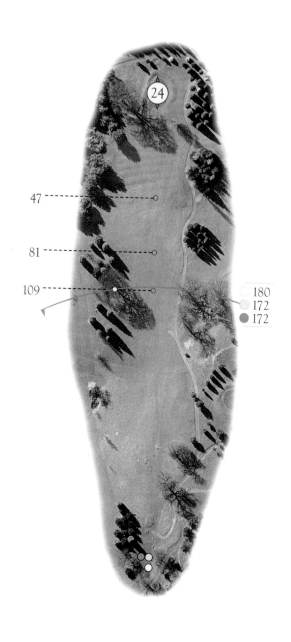

47 ----

81 ----

109 ----

○ 180
◔ 172
● 172

12th Hole - Par 4 - 301 yards

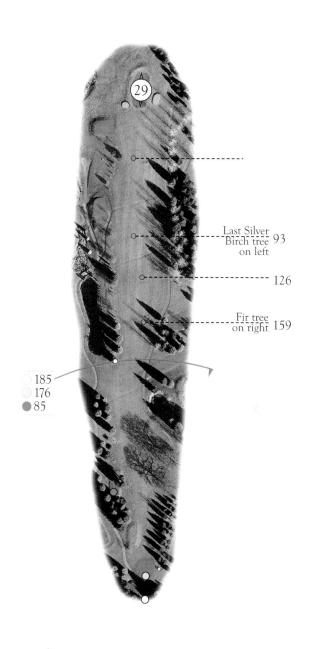

13th Hole - Par 3 - 190 yards

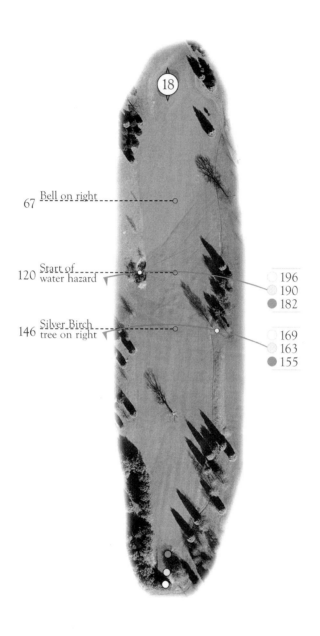

67 Bell on right

120 Start of
water hazard

196
190
182

146 Silver Birch
tree on right

169
163
155

14th Hole - Par 4 - 308 yards

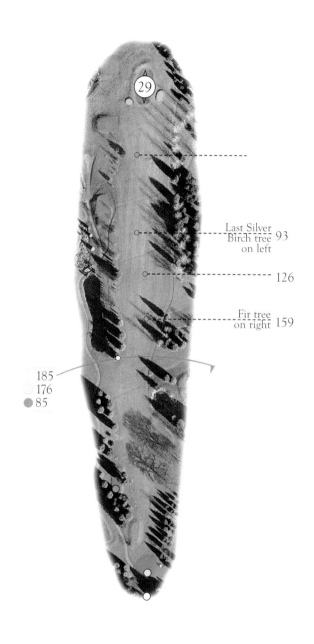

Last Silver
Birch tree 93
on left

126

Fir tree
on right 159

185
176
85

15th Hole - Par 5 - 477 yards

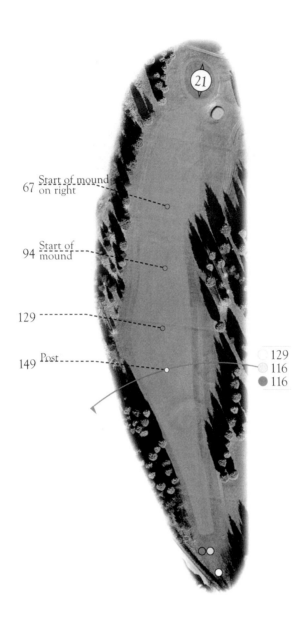

16th Hole - Par 4 - 310 yards

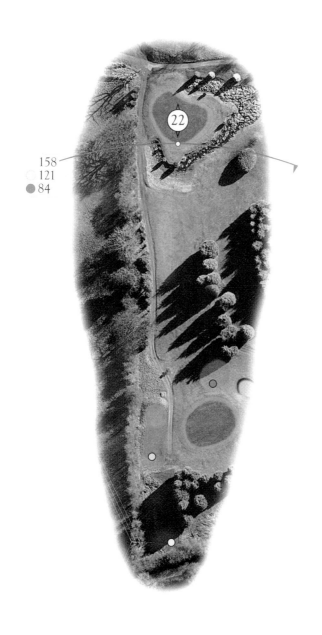

158
121
84

17th Hole - Par 3 - 169 yards

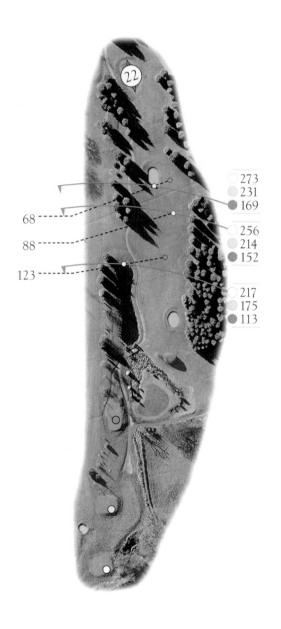

18th Hole - Par 4 - 348 yards

Annual Dinner Party
given by Directors

1991 - Rose Grocott, Ray Grocott, Maureen Smith and Bill Smith.

*1989 - Doris Ankers (now Mayor of Whitchurch) with
her daughters.*

1994 - Michael Welch, Brian Lewis and Bob Davies.

1989 - Gileen Shuker and Margaret Brown.

*1994 - Alex Harding, Jean Peate, Norman Peate
and Les Welch.*

1991 - Robert Walker and Brian Lewis.

1990 - Mike Shuker, Alex Harding and Norman Peate.

*1991 - Albert Murphy, Albert Minshall, Maura Murphy
and Duncan Shepherd.*

1989 - Roy Hughes, Sue Higgs and Fred Higgs.

1991 - Terry Cieselski, Brian Peake and David Fisher.

1991 - Andy Griffiths, Carol and John Williams.

1991 - Sheila Whiston, Val Whiston, Leslie Huxley and Vin Huxley.

*1993 - Tony Minshall, Margaret Brown, Keith Brown
and Jack Brown.*

1992 - Neil Humphreys, Tina Humphreys and Andrew Minshall.

1995 - Back: Henry Harding, Frank Speakes and John Bayley. Front: Pat Roberts, Dave Roberts, Ann Speakes, Leslie Huxley and Vin Huxley.

EPILOGUE

"You can't boast about what you've done because it's all here. I didn't build all this. I didn't design the trees. I didn't make the water or make the seeds for the grass. God did all that. We work together. I'm just a general manager for a lifetime, just for a wonderful lifetime."

Albert Minshall

POSTSCRIPT

"Well, it's probably all a load of old rubbish but you might get something out of it."

Albert Minshall
2006

Genesis 2: 2-3

By the seventh day God had finished the work he had been doing; so on the seventh day he rested from all his work. And God blessed the seventh day and made it holy, because on it he rested from all the work of creating he had done.

ACKNOWLEDGEMENTS

I would like to thank everyone who helped in the compilation of this book. Thank you for all your stories and anecdotes and for the good humour, willingness and generosity of spirit that I encountered from every person I met. Thank you for searching out and kindly lending me your photographs and newspaper cuttings. Everyone who contributed in any way, large or small, made the research and writing of this book a good experience, full of humour, warmth and just a bit of nostalgia for old days too!

I would particularly like to thank Garry Bailey for his initial text work that gave me good inspiration in the beginning; Tony Parsonage for his text work (Tee 5) and for reading through my text, in particular checking all the historical facts about golf; Margaret Hiles for such detailed and extensive archive press and photographs about Hill Valley from its opening days; Anthony Smith for compiling and giving me such accurate and detailed information about the club membership; Bob Walker for all the photographs he rooted out from all over Hill Valley as it was being demolished and re built around him, and smiling through it all the time. John Williams for stories, photographs and cuttings about the juniors. Alex de Barro for club information.

The Shropshire Star and Whitchurch Herald for permission to re-print photographs.

Kelly Lowe for her patience and time scanning photographs and generally answering so many of my questions through the months.

Finally and with great thanks to Hazel Willdigg for endless help and patience, always making me feel so welcome in her office and without exception looking after me so well.

Thank you to all of you who agreed to be interviewed and contribute your part to the book. Albert said to me at the beginning that the book must not contain, 'anything boastful nor anything against anybody'. The story of Hill Valley and Albert's role in its creation is brought to life in your own voices, as you saw it all unfold and play its part in all your lives through the years.

Gillian Lee